Mary Warnock is a philosopher. She has been fellow and tutor in philosophy at St Hugh's College, Oxford; headmistress of Oxford High School; and Mistress of Girton College, Cambridge. She sits as an independent life peer in the House of Lords, and published *Mary Warnock, A Memoir – People & Places* with Duckworth.

What the critics said:

'The chief value of this book [is that] it does not present final answers to every moral dilemma. How could it?
'What it does, rather, is show what it is like to think through moral questions with care, seriousness and an honest determination not to trivialise or simplify the horribly complicated issues they raise. In that sense, even if one disagreed with every moral opinion expressed in it, it would remain one of the best guides to ethics available.'
Ray Monk, *Sunday Telegraph*

'It is hard to believe that Mary Warnock's humane, lucid, honest and personal voice will not be attractive to anyone interested in the questions she discusses … The point of a book like this is to stimulate discussion in a clear-headed and serious way; in this it has plainly succeeded.'
Garrett Cullity, *Times Literary Supplement*

'Warnock's new book admirably fulfils the brief of its title. … This book fearlessly tackles a host of the favourite topics of pub bores. … This book will serve as an excellent introduction to ethical study, and is also an impassioned and moving summary of Warnock's own lifelong dedication to ethical thinking.'
Alain de Botton, *Guardian*

An Intelligent Person's
Guide to Ethics

An Intelligent Person's Guide to Ethics

Mary Warnock

Duckworth Overlook

London • New York • Woodstock

This edition 2004
First published in 1998 by
Duckworth Overlook

LONDON
90-93 Cowcross Street
London EC1M 6BF
inquiries@duckworth-publishers.co.uk
www.ducknet.co.uk

NEW YORK
The Overlook Press
141 Wooster Street
New York, NY 10012

WOODSTOCK
The Overlook Press
One Overlook Drive
Woodstock, NY 12498
www.overlookpress.com
[for individual orders and bulk sales in the United States,
please contact our Woodstock office]

A CIP catalogue record for this book is available from the
British Library and the Library of Congress

ISBN 0 7156 3320 1 (UK)
ISBN 1-58567-693-4 (US)

Typeset by Ray Davies
Printed in Great Britain by
CPD Ltd, Wales

Contents

Introduction

A guide to ethics might be thought to be a kind of hand-book on how to behave properly, like a guide to etiquette, or the Highway Code. Useful though such a book might be, it is not possible to write it. Ethics is a complicated matter. It is partly a matter of general principles, or even rules, like those of manners; but largely a matter of judge-ment and decision, of reasoning and sentiment, of having the right feeling at the right time, and every time is different. Above all it is a matter of trying to be a particu-lar sort of person. And though ethics (or moral philoso-phy, as I prefer to call it), like the rest of philosophy, has been secularised, it is almost impossible to think about the origins and development of morality itself without think-ing about its interconnections with religion. My own background is a small illustration of this.

My mother, though not pious, and disliking conven-tional piety, had had a very pious background, in that her grandmother, a German, had married into another German family that had converted to Christianity from Judaism. Religion was serious. My mother took church-going for granted, and having been a public schoolmaster's wife (my father died before I was born), she also took for granted not just Sunday attendance, but bells summoning one to chapel every day. The liturgy was something I grew up with, and cathedral services were a source of endless pleasure and fascination. I went to an exceptionally religious school, St Swithun's, in Winchester, first by day, then as a boarder, where it was assumed that the true purpose of school was to make us good. The school motto was *Caritas Humilitas Sinceritas*; and the adolescence of myself and my friends was engaged largely with the contemplation of the last of these virtues. We endlessly examined ourselves and one another to find out whether we had really meant what we said or were only showing off; whether we really liked the things we professed to like, despised those things we claimed to, or whether these sentiments too were insincere. Though we may often have behaved badly, there is no doubt that we wanted to be good. I did not realise how important a fact this was until much later. But I do remember one day at school, just before I left, coming to a sudden realisation that nothing was or could ever be truly intolerable except the recognition that one had behaved badly in some serious, non-trivial matter.

When I went to Oxford the moral pressure and the religious atmosphere lifted. While I was reading Classical Honour Moderations almost the only pressure I was under was the pressure to work, to try to improve the lamentable standard of my girls' school Latin and Greek and try to justify the scholarship which I had won, I knew, entirely by pretending to be brighter than I was, and getting away with it. It was 1942 when I started as an undergraduate, and so there was a wartime assumption of collective righteousness, of being on the right side, strengthened in my case by my friendship with Elisabeth de Gaulle, the General's daughter, who was reading history in my year at college. The atmosphere was not so much moralistic as heroic.

After Oxford, having completed the first half of my degree course, and starting when I was just twenty, I taught for two years at a more relaxed girls' school than mine had been, Sherborne School for Girls. But the horrors of the Holocaust became generally known at this time, and I reflected for the first time that humans have a great deal in common: I could not be sure that I did not have instincts as detestable as those of the Nazis, nor that I would have had the clarity of vision or the strength of character to resist these instincts, had I been a German at the time. I remember a particularly awful insight, that I, though I knew myself to be a good class teacher, was capable of being a bully, and tormenting a child if she irritated me, or seemed generally contemptible. The purpose of morality, I thought, must surely be to make one constantly alert to such temptations.

So when I went back to Oxford I was prepared to be interested in moral philosophy, a compulsory subject in Greats. In the event, I quite enjoyed it, but nothing like as much as I enjoyed working for the epistemology paper, or Plato and Aristotle (also concerned largely with moral philosophy, but a wonderfully alien and non-Christian morality, where the fascination was translation, seeing, that is, whether there was any way to render the Greek concepts of ethics intelligible, without ingrained Christian vocabulary and outlook being allowed to creep in). I think the main reason for my rather lukewarm attention to moral philosophy was that at the time (1946-1948) it was, as a subject, in very poor shape in Oxford. No one was prepared to take it, or its relation, political philosophy, seriously. The explanation for this was twofold. First, at the beginning of the century, G.E. Moore, a celebrated Cambridge philosopher, had written an undeservedly influential book, *Principia Ethica*, in which he purported to show that moral judgements were based on an infallible and simple intuitive knowledge of what things were good. The things that were good, friendship, for example, or the contemplation of beauty, were just obviously so, to anyone who thought about the matter clearly. A moral decision between two possible courses of action must therefore be based on a calculation as to which of the two would bring about more of these manifestly good things. If two people disagreed about what, as a matter of ethics, they ought to do, they were simply disagreeing about which possible course of action would have the consequence that more of the indisputably good things would come into existence. They could not disagree about what was good. This was Moore's startling and simplistic solution to the problems of morality. He was the guru of the Bloomsbury group, and it is hard not to think that he owed his undoubted fame more to his personality (his solemnity, his highly emphatic way of speaking, his obvious integrity, and his manifest purity of character) than to his arguments. For on the whole he did not use arguments in *Principia Ethica*. He simply asserted things.

But there was one argument which he deployed, and which was the subject of endless debate. He accused John Stuart Mill, in his *Utilitarianism*, a text much read both then and now in courses on moral philosophy, of committing what he called the Naturalistic Fallacy. Mill, he alleged, did not realise the great gulf between *moral* judgements, the subject of direct and infallible intuition of the good, simple, and incapable of further analysis, and complex judgements of *fact*, such as that people prefer pleasure to pain. Mill, he said, obscured, indeed denied the difference between the desirable and the desired, between what people do want, and what it is good that they should want. This argument was an object of great fascination to later philosophers and we spent much time in our undergraduate essays discussing it. But in our hands it was an argument concerned exclusively with different *kinds of proposition*, propositions of fact and propositions of value. A proposition of fact might be that it was raining, while a proposition of value would be that rain is good for the crops. It did not much matter what examples you took to illustrate the difference, so long as you acknowledged it. As for the content of morality, what moral judgements were actually about, though we perhaps realised that Moore's choice of intrinsically good things was rather one-sided, we seldom considered the part of his book where he laid out what these good things were (the part that must most have impressed the members of the Bloomsbury group). Even if we had discussed it, there would not have been much to say: for according to Moore either you agreed with his list of intrinsic and unanalysable good things, or you had not thought about it properly. Either you saw what things were good or you were blind. In any case, we, as budding philosophers, were not supposed to be concerned with actual good and evil, harm and benefit, but only with the nature of the language in which such things were discussed by others, not engaged in philosophy. They, we were taught, were concerned with 'first-order' morality. We, elevated above the fray, dealt with 'second-order' topics; not with what is the case, but with the analysis of the language in which the non-philosophical seek to express what is the case.

The other, related influence which accounted for the low standing of moral philosophy came to the same sort of conclusion from a different route, and made it equally impossible to discuss real ethical problems that might arise in the real world. This was the aftermath of logical positivism, which had burst on the English-speaking world from Vienna, just before the war. Logical positivism held as its central dogma that 'the meaning of a proposition is its method of verification'; that is to say that unless you could verify or falsify a statement, it was strictly meaningless, indeed it was only masquerading as a statement. There were, it was true, other statements, those of mathematics or logic, that were held to have meaning, since to assert them was to assert either a necessary truth or a contradiction. But apart from these, only statements of verifiable fact had meaning. It followed that all statements of the form 'stealing is wrong' or 'God is love' were pseudo-statements, pretending to state facts, but actually meaningless. A.J. Ayer, whose youthful and exuberant book, *Language, Truth and Logic*, had introduced these theories to the English-speaking world in 1936, held that such pseudo-propositions were expressions of emotion, like the hissing or slow hand-clapping you might use to evince your disapproval of a performance in the opera house. You could say, 'Many people assert that God is love' or 'Most people believe that stealing is wrong', for such propositions could be verified by the counting of heads. But to go further, and declare either of these propositions directly, would be to speak nonsense.

Not much philosophy had been seriously discussed during the war, most philosophers having left their universities for other things. So when they came back, it was widely taken for granted that the statements of ethics (that something was right or that it was wrong, that something was courageous or that it was cowardly) as well as most statements of politics (that such and such would be a right policy to adopt) were strictly meaningless, and not worth discussing. What was permitted was to discuss what kind of uses (since they could not have the 'proper' use of statements, to convey factual information) such statements might be allowed to have: to persuade, for instance, or to emote.

The consequence was that moral and political philosophy

became curiously easy subjects. We had to read the classical texts of the subject, Hume, Locke, Kant and Moore (apart from Plato and Aristotle). But we had not really to engage with what they said, for we were taught that they said nothing significant. They were analysing, or justifying, something, namely ethics, which had only a fake existence. Apart from reading the texts, our task was to show that the Naturalistic Fallacy was indeed a fallacy; for logical positivism had introduced it by another route from Moore's. The distinction between fact and value, we thought, had been once and for all uncovered and remained absolute. Philosophers, professionally speaking, having recognised and elaborated this distinction, had no more right to pontificate about what things actually were valuable than anyone else. It was not our business. No wonder we were often referred to as ourselves logical positivists, though we had given up, or never adopted, the general tenets of that philosophy.

I am far from decrying the kind of linguistic philosophy practised in Oxford after the war. Indeed I think it absolutely central to philosophy to explore the language of perception, the language we use to speak of our personal identity, how our concepts of space and time are incorporated in the communication we have with other humans, and many more such topics, which make up epistemology, philosophical logic and metaphysics. But, I began to believe, this is not the whole of philosophy. There are questions that must be asked about values, what we value and why, and who 'we' are when we are inclined to raise these problems. I would not have put it like this, at the time. It would have sounded too pretentious. The word 'value' was thoroughly discredited. It was used, as I have said, to distinguish different kinds of propositions (those dealing with facts being totally distinct from those dealing with values). But apart from that it was out of favour. It suggested too much the pieties of the war which we had got sick of hearing. For it has to be remembered that after the war our mood was iconoclastic; there were balloons to be pricked and their deflation was extremely good sport. All the same I personally began to feel discontented with the triviality of linguistic philosophy, as applid to ethics.

At the end of the 1950s, when I had been teaching philosophy for nearly ten years, I was asked by the Oxford University Press whether I would contribute a volume to the Home University Library to be entitled *Ethics Since 1900*. It is symptomatic of the status of moral philosophy at that time that two people had been asked already and had turned it down, and all three of us were women. Soft options for the girls was certainly then the general feeling. Rather at the last minute the General Editor of the Home University Library rang up to say that there was this thing called existentialism, and this chap called Sartre, and perhaps I ought to include a chapter on this in the book, to set it apart from other current histories of the subject. I had never read a word of Sartre, though his plays and novels were spoken of, and indeed I had heard, and been enormously impressed by, *Huis Clos* more than ten years before, when it was chosen as part of the first night of the

BBC Third Programme. My heart sank, but I agreed to do it, and to try to do it by the end of the Long Vacation, just beginning. So for a cold and windy summer I sat on the beach at Sandsend on the North Yorkshire coast (where we had a holiday house), crouching behind a wind-shield while our then four children dammed the stream, and I read *L'Etre et le Néant*. I hated it, and in many ways I still do. I hated the solemnity, the highly French pretentiousness, the wordiness, the neologisms, the sheer weight of gobbledegook. (I was not to know that later, in the days of Foucault and Derrida, Sartre would come to look like a model of clarity and economy.) But I realised, at the same time, that here was a kind of philosophy completely different from the purely 'second order' moral philosophy of Oxford. It was hands-on.

For one thing it was, in part, unashamedly *metaphysical*, deriving morality from the nature of the universe and man's place in it, in the manner of Plato and Spinoza, philosophers to whom I was greatly addicted. A not very elevated role for morality emerged from this: morality is nothing but self-deception. There is no such thing as an absolute value. All values are relative and invented. Humans, being at a distance from the world of *things* because of their powers of reflection on these, themselves unthinking, things, are always trying to pretend that they, men themselves, are absolutely thing-like, bound by duties and obligations, just as material objects are bound by the laws of gravity. Men are made sick and dizzy by the thought of their own freedom; so they deny it.

Secondly, the arguments in support of this thesis were not arguments at all, but anecdotes. The method was largely a narrative method, stories told so vividly that you could not but believe in the vignette. For example, to make the point central to his thought that humans deceive themselves, pretending to an inevitability in their lives when in fact they can live them as they choose, pretending they are bound by obligations which in fact they invent for themselves and can perfectly well disregard, Sartre tells the story of a waiter who claims that he *has to* get up at five and open the café, that he cannot but sweep the floor, obsequiously attend to his clients, and so on. He is all the time playing, and over-playing his part. He is pretending to be a waiter, body and soul. This story is so brilliantly told that one cannot argue with the conclusion. One simply recognises the *man in bad faith*. When Sartre embarks on the narrative mode, at once all the pretentiousness and obscurity are dispelled, and the point is made.

I wrote in my ethics book, published in 1960,* that the subject had become trivialised, but that I believed the most boring days were over. In a new edition in 1977, I wrote a postscript in which I said that my faith had been justified. Real subjects were now the proper concern of moral philosophers. The only threat to the subject that I could then see was a kind of creeping relativism which morality itself, let alone moral philosophy, could not survive. I shall return to the subject.

In 1977, when the postscript was written, I was spend-

* *Ethics Since 1900*

ing much of my time chairing a government enquiry into the education of children with disabilities, referred to in our final report as children with special educational needs. It was, I think, the first time that I had publicly to justify a particular moral standpoint to a general, and especially a parliamentary, readership. For, though most of the report was concerned with organisational and curricular matters, right at the beginning of the report we had to make, and agree to, a moral statement. The circumstances in which the committee was set up made such a moral statement imperative. Until the early 1970s, children with very severe and multiple disabilities had been denied education. They were offered care and sometimes therapy, but they were deemed ineducable. But in 1972 the right of all children to education was established by law, and for the first time severely disabled children were brought within the general framework of education, the responsibility not of the Department of Health but of the Department of Education, which already looked after the less severely disabled. One man was largely responsible for this change, an immensely enthusiastic, resourceful and compassionate man called Stanley Segal, who died in 1995. He wrote a book called *No Child is Ineducable*, sent a copy to every Member of Parliament, and lobbied mercilessly until the change came about. This was how it was that our committee was set up, by the then Secretary of State, Margaret Thatcher. There were two philosophical questions that the committee had to address, before getting down to the details. The first was What is the purpose of education? Is it really plausible to use the word at all in connection with children so severely mentally and physically retarded that they cannot sit up or feed themselves or ever hope to speak? The second was How can one justify spending very large sums of money on education for those who by ordinary standards will never benefit from it, and certainly never repay the money spent by contributing to society, but will continue to need support all their lives?

In an attempt to answer the first question I can distinctly remember a weekend meeting, at a dismal hotel in Surrey, when I saw a mental picture (it seemed to arise spontaneously as if in a dream, and indeed I may well have been half asleep) which would help to answer the question, and I set about to present this image to the committee. I saw that education was a road down which every child had to walk, but there was only one road, with a common destination. At the end of the road lay the common goals: understanding of the world, enjoyment of it, and the independence that would empower the child to control it. Some children would have a smooth and easy passage down the road, but for others there would be formidable obstacles. Some would emerge fully equipped to understand, enjoy and control. Others would progress very little way towards the shared goals. But in their case every step counted. These children would have to be helped to surmount the obstacles one by one, and the need for help, often to do things, like talking, which other children learn to do without effort, was where the concept of 'special needs' came from. I, and I think we all, came away from this otherwise horrible weekend feeling that we had achieved not only clarity (up to a point), but some sort of shared and shareable vision, as well as a handy title for our report, and, as it turned out, for subsequent legislation.

But there remained the other question. What was to be the justification for spending such huge sums of money on educating children who were not going to get very far, and who certainly would not repay the expenditure by their contributions to the economy? (Such questions became far more urgent later, in the days of the Thatcher Government, but they were already asked.) The short answer and one which I found I deeply believed in was 'equality'. Of course one could have given an answer in terms of equal rights; since the law was changed in 1972, these children, all children, had an equal right to be educated. But that would somehow have begged the question. We felt we needed not merely to appeal to the law, as it newly was, but to justify that law: to explain why it was morally right that the law *had* been changed. And so we had to fall back on the statement that all children are equally human. But even among members of the committee, all of whom, it must be remembered, were concerned, at a practical level, in the education of the disabled, there were nevertheless some who said that all children were not equally human. Some were 'vegetables'. I found myself shocked by this metaphor; and I thought how easy and satisfactory it would be to respond with another metaphor, that all were God's children. Such language, however, has no place in an official report, and rightly. For one has to find arguments which do not rely on dogma accepted by some and not by others. And this is as true of philosophy as it is of government reports. Yet the desire I felt to counter the horticultural metaphor with one derived, as it were, from the Garden of Eden showed me something that I had not recognised before in my professional capacity, namely how powerful the metaphors of religion are, and how one may find them, in some circumstances, virtually indispensable. In the end we reinforced the argument from equality (not an unexamined dogma, but a shared value) with the argument we had used before, the argument derived from the image of the single road. It makes more difference for a child who cannot speak, and does not know even how to communicate by pointing, to be taught the meaning of pointing, and so to be granted a little bit of independent choice (even if the choice is only between chocolate and raspberry Angel Delight), than it does for a talented child to choose whether to learn the violin or the French horn. The change in the direction of understanding, enjoyment and control is, for the disabled child, immense, small though the steps may be.

I have cited this example at some length, because it illustrates what has come to seem to me an enormously important part of the task of moral philosophers, to try to engender practical understanding. I do not believe that you can make moral judgements unless, as far as possible, you know what you are talking about. Therefore in real situations you have to take care to find out as much as you can about the facts, from experts. I do not believe either that you can make good decisions unless you bring to bear on them a general understanding of the ethical issues involved. It is here that the moral philosopher may be of some use, in demonstrating what it is to adopt an ethical point of view.

The work of this committee also opened my eyes to a distinction about which I was not, and probably am not, wholly clear, though it is of the last importance. We must distinguish, though not absolutely, public from private morality. I have come to believe, from working on the committee I have just discussed and other committees which addressed other moral issues, that the relation between private morality, the dictates of conscience, if one may put it so, and a public policy that is democratically acceptable, seen widely to be decent, is a subtle and complicated interrelation. But we must try to get it right, otherwise we shall be dominated for ever by the ethics of the pub bore, who will say, 'I think it's disgusting. There ought to be a law against it.'

The pub bore speaks intuitively. (He is perhaps a coarse version of G.E. Moore, though Bloomsbury might shun the analogy.) Even if he has good reasons for his judgement that something is 'disgusting', he may not be able to articulate them (just as one may recognise someone immediately from a distance, without necessarily being able to say what it was about him that made him so recognisable). His conclusion, that the thing is wrong, may be perfectly sound. But he makes the false assumption that his judgement should, or could, be instantly translated into a law which should govern everyone, and turn that which he is objecting to into a criminal offence. When people become legislators or politicians, they assume new responsibilities. They have specifically to exercise reason and caution in attempting to foresee the consequences for everyone, including minority groups, of the measures they are proposing. This is not to say that they can be wholly Machiavellian, putting on one side the sensibilities of morality for the sake of successful rule. But it is to suggest that there is a number of kinds of moral judgements or decisions that they are not entitled to make, decisions that a private person might make out of friendship, love, or a desire for self-sacrifice, or indeed out of shame or outrage. Moreover, they owe a duty to be able to explain why they have come to the conclusion they have. They must be seen to have thought rationally; and in public circumstances this means that they be seen to have thought about the long-term consequences of what it is they propose. They must be seen to be steady and consistent in the stance they take, not only because they will probably advance their own careers if so perceived, but because steady and principled government is what is actually needed by society. So the overlap, or interplay, between the public and the private comes at the place where principles are to be articulated, and the consequences for society as a whole openly taken into account. In the sphere of public morality it is not enough simply to say, 'I feel I must' do this or that, except in the case where the public and private conflict. A public figure who resigns over a conscience issue is entitled to say, 'I can no other.' But public morality as such must be explained, and explained with reference to a common good. All these things I began to learn from my experiences at the Department of Education and I will deal with them in this book.

Death

To show how important the interrelation between public and private ethics is, as well as to show how ethical issues spring up all round one in real life, I want to tell two unoriginal, but more or less fictitious, stories about controlling the timing of death. Euthanasia is a topic which, as no one could deny, poses specifically moral dilemmas, dilemmas which, these days, it is a recognised part of ethics, or moral philosophy, to discuss, though it would have been beyond the narrow pale of discussion in the 1940s and 1950s.

The first story is this: there is a woman who is terminally ill, that is to say her life cannot last for more than two or three months. She is in great distress, because her illness progressively affects her ability to breathe. She has lost so much weight that she is, literally, painfully thin. She is too weak to be able to move herself, and she is entirely dependent on her husband, and the nurses who come in every day. She is given analgesics, including morphia, which marginally ease her breathing. But she longs to die, as she knows she soon will. She longs to release her husband from his terrible life, and she has had enough of her own. The consultant whom she used to see at an earlier stage of her illness has indicated that there is no more treatment he can give, and so she, and her husband, are looked after by their GP. He calls on them at frequent intervals, at least twice a week, and has become a friend. She is terrified of dying of suffocation, and has told both her husband and her doctor this; for such a death has always been a nightmare to her, and now she cannot sleep for thinking about it. When she does sleep, she wakes from a nightmare of suffocation. One day they are talking about it, the three of them together, and the doctor says to her, 'You shall not die by suffocating. I promise.' She is enormously relieved, and sleeps well that night, suffering no nightmares. The next day the doctor privately tells her husband that he is gradually increasing the dosage of morphia. Nothing further is said, but both the doctor and the husband know what is implied. Within a few weeks, the woman has died.

The second story is entirely different. A young girl, still in her teens, has suffered horrendous head injuries from the collapse of the building in which she works where a bomb had been placed. She is rescued from the rubble after many hours, and is taken unconscious to hospital. After several days in intensive care, it becomes apparent that she is capable of breathing without support, and her digestive system is working properly, but she is in a coma. So she remains for many weeks, while brain scans are taken, and every possible examination of the state of her brain is carried out. She shows no signs of consciousness at all, though she can move a little, and may move her head slightly if an intense light is flashed. But she does not respond to quite painful stimuli, such as pin-pricks, and she has no sense of hearing or of normal visual stimuli. After a year, she is said to be in a Permanent Vegetative State (PVS), which means that though she is not dead, according to the ordinary brain-stem death criterion, yet the rest of her brain is entirely useless to her, being, for the most part, a mass of fluid. In order to keep her alive, she needs food and drink, which are administered to her through tubes to the stomach. She has constant nursing attention as well, for the prevention of bedsores. Her parents, who visit her every day and have tried every kind of stimulus to arouse her, as well as her boyfriend, who also visits, want her to die, arguing that she is dead already as far as they are concerned. They know that she is not suffering, but that she will not recover, and, with the nursing care she is getting, may live for twenty or thirty more years. The hospital, however, do not believe that they can deliberately kill her by a lethal injection, for fear that the doctor who administered the injection might be held on a charge of murder; nor do they think they can, ethically, let her die of starvation and dehydration. And so they take the case to court. It is a very odd case: the judge is required to decide whether, if they did certain things, or omitted certain things, they would be committing murder. They have so far committed no crime. At last, after a long-drawn-out hearing and an appeal, the case ends in the House of Lords, where the Law Lords judge that the girl may be allowed to die, nutrition and hydration being withdrawn.

Both my stories, different though they are, pose in the end the same ethical problem. Ought the doctors to have intervened as they did, with the result that the two women died when they did? Or ought they to have 'allowed nature to take its course'? (Though we must note that 'nature taking its course' seems to mean, if it means anything, different things in the two stories.)

We will start with the first story. There are various essential elements in it, which will contribute to the moral judgement of the doctor's actions. The woman is 'naturally' ill; she has not suffered an accident, she has not been linked up to any life-support machines. Everything possible has been done for her that could be done. Her disease was diagnosed by means of a lung biopsy, and its progress was slowed down by means of drugs. Plainly this means that there has already been intervention of a kind that would not have been possible fifty or even twenty-five years ago. If nature had really been allowed to take its course, then she would have been dead long ago. The difference is that this was intervention with the aim of prolonging her life, and so is taken for granted. Yet it is worth noticing how slippery and evanescent our concept of the 'natural' is. Those who, for example, object to the idea of curing genetic diseases by means of gene manipulation on the grounds that it is 'unnatural' should perhaps, on the same grounds, object to curing appendicitis by means of surgery. We tend to regard as 'natural' those medical interventions to which we are accustomed, and which are often successful. Nothing could be less 'natural' than a plastic hip joint. Yet hip replacement surgery is seldom objected to on the apparently ethical grounds that it is contrary to nature.

The next crucial factor in the story is that the woman and her husband love each other, and therefore each can enter into the other's feelings and discern where each other's interests lie. The wife, quite apart from her own discomfort, pain and fear, is also distressed by the constrictions placed on her husband's freedom through her dependence on him. He is prepared for this sacrifice, but fully understands that his wife does not like to see him sacrificing himself. Neither of them has ever adopted the role of martyr or slave. Far beyond that, he is moved by his love and sympathy for her. Yet there is an asymmetry between them. She, quite without hesitation and with absolute sincerity, can say that she wants to die. He feels instant guilt at harbouring the thought that he wants her to die, even though he believes that to die would be in her own interest. She has nothing to gain from a life of increasing fear, breathlessness and pain. Each day is more horrible than the last, especially as she has an absolute understanding of what her situation is. Yet he believes that, much though he sympathises with her wish, if it becomes *his* wish, then it must be selfish. If he wants her to die this must be, deep down, because it is in his own interest that she should. And we arc taught, from childhood, that we should never wish someone else dead.

There is another element, a factor to which husband and wife may give different weight, according to their temperament. The wife, let us say, always placed a high value on independence and making her own choices. She now finds that, though she wants to die, she cannot choose to do so. For she cannot see how to die. Suicide would seem a proper choice; but she cannot commit suicide. She is too helpless. Nor can she bring herself to ask her husband to help her, because this would be to make him commit a crime. She is no longer in any sense autonomous; and her dependence is an enormous addition to her burdens. He too may, in principle, value autonomy. He may half wish that things were as they are in the Netherlands, when choosing death may really be an option for the terminally ill. Yet together they had watched a film about voluntary death in the Netherlands, and together they had agreed that neither of them could face the thought of deciding, 'Tonight's the night.' But in any case they live in Britain, not the Netherlands. They seem locked in a position from which there is no escape, which offers no plan that they can decide on and put into practice. Imminent, expected death produces a kind of paralysis. And death is so final, and so infinitely significant for the dying person, that to choose it for oneself may seem somehow to trivialise it.

The doctor understands all of this. He understands the husband's guilty feelings (which he knows will be, temporarily at least, extreme after his wife's death, whether she dies 'naturally' or not) and his agony at witnessing his wife's distress and degeneration. He understands, equally, the wife's horror at her inability to breathe and her weakness. He regards it as his duty as her doctor to make her inevitable death as easy as he can. Hence his promise to her. He understands that when his patients, as they come to grasp their own approaching death, say, 'I know that you will make it all right,' they do not mean that they believe he will find a cure, but that they believe he will not let dying be too horrible. However, he also knows that even voluntary euthanasia, where the patient has actually expressed a wish, even a longing, to die, is against the law; that intentionally killing someone is murder, the most serious crime there is, and punishable by mandatory life imprisonment (and incidentally no one who has been convicted of such an offence, a mercy killing, over the last decade has served less than six years of his sentence). And here plainly the doctor, in weighing up all the considerations, is moving from the consideration of private to public morality.

Let us try to divide all the elements listed above, the factors which will prove relevant to the final moral judgement, according to the private/public dichotomy. We will find that it will not work perfectly; but where there are overlaps, the complications of the issue will become the more apparent.

I must first make clear what I mean by 'private morality'. I most certainly do not mean a morality consciously made up by someone for his own use, a set of principles deliberately adopted by someone who says, 'This is how

I ought to live; it is my own plan, and it applies to no one else but me.' Such a set of principles might, I suppose, be adopted (rather as a nun takes her vows) but it must be rare. And if the set of principles were really supposed to have no application or relevance to anyone else at all, then it is doubtful whether it would be properly thought of as a morality. There are, after all, many instances of rules by which one lives, or tries to live, which are nothing to do with ethics. (I, for example, make it a rule to pay bills as soon as I get them. But this is a safeguard against forgetting to pay them at all, or losing them among the silt on my desk, combined with a purely personal horror of debt. Though adherence to this rule may work out generally ethically better than the habit of being slow to pay, it is not adopted for ethical reasons.) When I speak of private morality, on the contrary, I mean a morality grounded in a mixture of principle and sentiment, from whatever source these come, which together give rise to an imperative for the person who experiences the mixture. It may be quite narrow in its scope. It may be felt, for example, in determining how one must treat one's friends or one's children and may not in any sense suggest a scheme of how one should live one's entire life. It is the outcome of what in the eighteenth century was called moral sense, and it is frequently felt as sympathy, compassion or pity, or, it might be, as loyalty, or as shame at the thought of deceiving someone, or breaking a promise. I shall try to analyse this potent moral force at a later stage. For the time it is enough to say that the characteristic of 'private morality' is that it rests on a feeling that I must do, or refrain from doing, something, never mind the consequences, or what prudence might dictate.

In our first story, those who are most deeply involved, the woman and her husband, are obsessed with the question What is it right for us to do? as a matter of private morality. For the woman, her desire to die arises from the awfulness of her life, as she experiences it. But part of that awfulness is the awareness of the burden she is placing on her husband, day by day and hour by hour. She feels that she *must* release him. Even if she did not want to die, she would still feel she ought to, for his sake. And here there emerges a truth about ethics. One cannot have a duty, or obligation, to oneself. Though people say things like, 'You owe it to yourself,' this is a not very happy metaphor carried over from what is the real context of duty, other people. This is the specifically ethical content of the woman's thinking. Her own misery cannot by itself give rise to the thought that she has a *duty* to die, only that she has a wish to. To satisfy that wish may become part of someone else's ethical imperative, but not of her own. Regarding her own misery, the furthest her ethical thinking may get is that it cannot be wrong to end it.

The husband, although, as we have seen, he cannot bring himself to say that he wishes her dead, is moved, first and foremost, by his intense sympathy with her sufferings. He cannot bear to witness them. Just as finding an animal caught in a trap may arouse such feelings of pity for the pain and the struggles of the animal that a moral imperative is generated – 'I *must* release it or destroy it. I *cannot* leave it to suffer' – so with his wife. He cannot allow the suffering to last.

There is another kind of argument which may count among the dictates of private morality, but this time probably on the other side, and that is the kind derived from a religious belief, personally held, as a matter of faith. There are various ways in which this argument may be formulated. It is often said that God gives life as a precious gift, so only God should take it away. As it stands, this seems to be a *non sequitur*. Normally, if someone gives you a present, it is yours either to keep or dispose of, though it may be bad manners too openly to dispose of it. A more plausible way of presenting the case is in terms not of gift but of loan, or of stewardship. You are given your life to make the most of it, and must hand it back in the end. But making the most of a life does not include bringing it to an end yourself, or permitting others to do so for you. Therefore to allow your life to be ended early by a doctor, even if you are on the brink of death, must be wrong. If you are tempted by your sufferings to beg for death, you must resist the temptation. This seems to me a heroic position to adopt. But it is a position which essentially depends on possessing a certain kind of faith. It would be hard to formulate its secular equivalent, unless perhaps in the form of a kind of obstinacy: 'I've started, so I'll finish,' 'I am not going to be defeated,' 'Death, be not proud.' It is sometimes formulated in terms of the *sanctity* of human life. I shall examine this concept in connection with our second story.

The doctor shares the husband's sympathy, but for him it is (because in the story he is a good doctor) compounded by a professional commitment to easing the sufferings of his patients. This does not, of course, mean that he will always kill his patients rather than have them suffer. Everything depends on the probable outcome of the suffering. But this does not change the nature of his duty. If a patient is in intense pain as a result of what is likely to be successful and beneficial surgery, his duty is still to ease the pain as much as possible, and not be careless of it. If a child patient is terrified of a treatment that is necessary, it is his duty to try to make the treatment tolerable, and soothe the child's fears. It is only in the case of the suffering of those who are certainly dying that the question of 'easing the passing', or hastening the end, arises. A GP, who might well be the doctor in the first story, recently put it thus: 'By the correct definition, we doctors are practising euthanasia all the time, and we should be proud of it ... My job is to ease suffering. That can prolong life; but if it brings death closer, that is irrelevant.' The doctor who wrote those words was expressing a personal conviction as to the ethics of the medical profession, his interpretation of his own duty. And though he plainly, in speaking of 'we doctors,' expected that his view of this duty was shared by his colleagues, nevertheless the imperative was felt as an imperative binding on him, immediately. Nor would he be able *not* to feel this duty weighing on him, however many of his colleagues disagreed.

As an aside, we may notice that the doctor whom I quoted above spoke about 'suffering', not 'pain'; and indeed he published his statement with specific reference to patients who suffered from increasing breathlessness, as the woman in the first story did. This is of importance only because this kind of euthanasia is often discussed in the context of inoperable cancers, or intractable pain of whatever origin. In the famous trial of Dr Bodkin Adams in 1957, one of the witnesses for the prosecution, a Dr Douthwaite, gave it as his settled opinion that drugs such as morphia and heroin, which had been used by Dr Adams to hasten the death of one of his elderly and dying patients, should not have been used 'even in the terminal stages' of an illness that was not an inoperable cancer.

> Mr L. (defence counsel): Is the sole difference between the two this, in your opinion, that in the cancer case the use of the drugs would be justified because of the presence of pain, and in the other case they are not justified because there was only severe distress, which falls short of severe pain?
>
> Dr D.: Yes. (Patrick Devlin, *Easing the Passing*, Bodley Head, 1985, p. 127.)

Things may have changed a little since the 1950s, but not very much. One is often told that euthanasia is unnecessary because pain can always be controlled. This seems to me not only probably untrue, but often irrelevant.

Besides his sympathy with his patient, and his own interpretation of his moral duty as a doctor, the doctor in the first story was also bound to consider, as we saw, the status of euthanasia under the law. And this is to change the question from one of private to one of public ethics. For the law has to govern the behaviour of everyone, and distinguish for everyone what is right or permissible from what is wrong and criminal. The law cannot take account of feelings, or motive (though sentencing policy should be able to do so). The law is concerned only with intention. Was there *mens rea* (guilty intent)? The woman and her husband also had to consider these public issues. The woman did not want to implicate either her husband or indeed her doctor in criminal activity. But I shall concentrate, in what follows, on the doctor's arguments. For it is part of his professionalism that he understand the law in the matter of euthanasia, that he act within the law, or, if he believed it right to do so, campaign for the law to be changed.

Now the doctor, as I have said, understands perfectly well that intentional killing is murder. Not only does he not wish to commit murder for the sake of his own life and career, but he also believes that murder is wrong. And yet in our story he deliberately increases the dosage of morphia until the woman dies. And the quoted, real-life, doctor wrote, 'We doctors are practising euthanasia all the time.' Many other doctors have been heard to say the same, and many, for example, testified to this effect in giving evidence to the 1995 House of Lords Select

Committee on Medical Ethics, which was set up to deal with two notorious cases of 'mercy-killing'.

The way such doctors let themselves off the hook when challenged is through the argument from double effect, an argument that has now been recognised as a way of distinguishing legitimate from illegitimate termination of life, both by the Vatican's *Declaration on Euthanasia*, and by the British Medical Association's ethical guidelines on the same subject. The argument turns on a distinction between foreseeing an outcome and intending it. So a doctor may claim that, in increasing a dose of morphia, his intention was to ease the suffering of his patient, although he also foresaw that this would in fact shorten her life. Her death would then be an '*unintended consequence*' of the increased dosage. And this is quite different, so the argument runs, from the doctor's quite deliberately administering a fatal injection, or even increasing the normal dosage gradually, with the express intention of causing the death of the patient. It seems that the doctor could deliberately perform the same action (increase the dosage) with two completely distinguishable intentions; the one a benign, the other a malicious or at least a culpable intention.

Even writing what I have just written, making explicit the argument from double effect, makes me uneasy. For, though I am extremely glad that it has become widely accepted that the doctor's behaviour in our first story is morally justifiable, and that such methods are acknowledged to be widely practised ('we doctors are practising

euthanasia all the time'), yet there seems something artificial and indeed Jesuitical about the argument itself and
the distinction on which it hinges. In ordinary life it is
extremely difficult to distinguish intending the act from,
thereby, intending the foreseen consequence. Very often,
if we are asked what we are doing, we include the expected outcome of our action in our answer to the
question, in describing, that is, the act itself. We hardly
ever, except as a joke, confine our answer to the action
itself. I am very unlikely, if asked what I am doing at the
dining-room table, to reply, 'I am putting a fork to the left
of a table-mat.' I am much more likely to say, 'I am laying
the table,' or 'I am preparing for my dinner-party.' Not
only am I acting intentionally, in putting the fork on the
table, but my intention covers many more actions and
intended outcomes. However, it may be argued that this
kind of example is irrelevant, because the whole activity,
up to and including the dinner-party, is, presumably,
blameless. The need to distinguish intention from outcome does not arise unless there arises also a need to
excuse oneself, and deny responsibility for an outcome
that would generally be seen as undesirable. Elizabeth
Anscombe, in a detailed analysis of the concept of intention, gives a variety of examples to illustrate how far one's
intention may stretch, and how one may, nevertheless, cut
it off at a particular point, with varying degrees of plausi-
bility (G.E.M. Anscombe, *Intention*, Blackwell, 1957).
For instance, a man has been hired to take responsibility
for keeping the drinking-water tank full for a family, in

the house they have rented for the holidays. He fully intends to carry out the duty for which he is being paid. Someone warns him that the water-supply has become seriously polluted. Nevertheless he continues to carry out his obligation to fill the tank, and the family is poisoned. Could he plausibly escape blame, by claiming that he was intentionally doing only what he was being paid to do, namely fill the tank? He did not intend to poison the family, he may have borne them no ill will, but knowing that the water was poisonous, he also knew what the consequences would be if they drank the water. The separation here between intention and foreseen consequence, even though it may be made in theory, seems in practice to be ethically positively monstrous.

Again, consider the following case: I am an amateur flautist, and I am about to give a rare solo performance tomorrow. I am deeply dissatisfied with my ability to carry out a particular trill evenly and expressively, and am determined to practise hard. I know that I have an elderly neighbour who is, as it happens, very ill at the moment, and is peculiarly sensitive to noise, as well as needing as much rest as possible. I also know that, even if I close all my windows, the sound of my practising can be heard through the wall. I go ahead and practise all the same. When I am reproached, I say, '*All I was doing* was perfecting my G sharp trill.' My intention was, as it were, exhausted by its direction towards a better performance the following day. The unwanted consequence, for which

I might indeed apologise, fell outside my intention. Why am I not off the moral hook, in this case?

In both the above examples it seems not only absurdly pedantic but morally reprehensible to attempt to separate the intention from the foreseen consequence of the act. If the agent knew what would, or was extremely likely to be, the outcome, then the meaning, the significance of his act might be summed up as 'poisoning the family' or 'preventing the neighbour from having her needed rest.' It is rather as if someone tried to separate out the meanings of individual words from the significance of a complete statement. Imagine the following dialogue:

A: The horse came towards you and you ran away.
B: I'm no coward. I'm not frightened of horses.
A: I never said you were frightened. I didn't say you ran away *because* the horse came towards you. All I said was the horse came towards you *and* you ran away.

But of course, though the word 'and' can be used, and often is used, just to list various items, as on a shopping list, without implying any connection between them, in the particular statement that A made, this is not the way 'and' is to be understood. We have to take the statement as a whole. So, it may seem, in real life we have to take people's actions and their consequences, when these are known, as a whole, and make sense of their actions as directed to the foreseen consequences.

Some doctors suggest that the double effect argument does not turn on our ability to distinguish intentions from foreseen consequences. For, they argue, you cannot foresee the effect of a particular dosage on a particular individual; therefore the doctor can never claim to *know* that the increased dose will shorten a patient's life; and they tell stories of patients who, given what would be assumed to be a lethal dose of morphia, wake up the following morning saying that they have had the best night's sleep they have had for years. Of course it is possible to use the word 'know' in this extremely limited way, so limited that you could never claim to know that something *would* happen, to 'foresee' it, only that it *had* happened. So words like 'dying' would cease to have any meaning. You could not claim to know that someone was dying, only that they had in fact died. Looking back, after he was dead, you could say, 'That was when he was dying,' but you could never confidently say, 'He *is* dying.' I think, however, that if doctors want to deny knowing that an increased dose will shorten life, then they will have to give up claiming to know all kinds of other things about which they will still want to make such a claim (as, indeed, that morphia will relieve pain, or make breathing easier, in the case of the woman in our story). So, for my part, I do not believe that this kind of modesty with regard to what can be foreseen will do anything to ease the doctor's ethical burden.

As I have said, I am thankful that it has become more and more generally recognised, and even by such hard-liners as the Vatican Council, that the argument from double effect will be accepted, and that doctors who deploy it will feel safe from prosecution. That does not prevent my regarding it as a very dubious and shifty argument, and one the use of which turns the attention away from the real point at issue. Moreover it has a fake exactitude. It pretends that we can and do know exactly where one intention ends and another begins. But an action, or plan of action, can be truthfully presented under so many descriptions, some narrower than others (e.g. 'What are you doing?' 'I'm putting a fork to the left of a mat,' or 'I'm getting ready for my dinner-party'), that no one description can be the only true description, and so no one intention can be the only real intention.

However, fortunately, it is more in theory than in practice, more in public and general policy statements than in private decisions and transactions, that the argument from double effect will be raised. Going back to our first story, it will be seen that no argument at all appeared. What he was doing was understood by the doctor and it was understood by the husband that that was what he was doing, and no argument, or rationalisation, was necessary. I believe that what happened was that the doctor made a value judgement: it was, at this stage of the woman's illness, *more important* that she should be relieved of her distress than that she should live an extra week, or even an extra month. And the husband concurred in this value judgement. If we look at the analogous stories, that of the man who poisoned the family, and of my persisting in practising my flute, it is clear that here, too, value judgements were made. The man whose job was to fill the drinking-water tank was so stupid or so self-absorbed that he judged it more important that he should do what he had contracted to do than that he should look beyond the narrow lines of his contractual duty to a wider duty, to protect the family from risk. Likewise I was so totally absorbed in the thought of the next day's performance that I had come to regard it as the most important thing in the world, other people's needs not being contenders. Nobody would be likely to exonerate either the tank-filling man or me, in my capacity as flautist, from the blame for what happened; and they certainly would not let us off, as I have argued, by the pretence that one can separate intention from foreseen and perhaps unwanted consequence. But because the doctor's action has what would generally be interpreted as a benign outcome, and because his motive (as distinct from his intention) is undoubtedly compassionate, he is allowed, in theory, to get away with a flawed argument.

However there are those, both among the general public and among doctors themselves, who do not regard the outcome, in our first story, as benign. As we saw, they may hold on religious grounds that it is not for the doctor or anyone else to take such action as will shorten someone's life, even by a few weeks, days or hours. Or, without appeal to any specific religious dogma, they may appeal to the sanctity of human life, the principle that deliberately to kill someone, or deliberately to take action that will result in their death, is always wrong; and that this is the moral point of the criminal law in respect of murder.

Whatever the quality of her life, whether painful or in other ways unbearable, and whether she has a short or a long time to live, it is simply wrong, in our story, that the woman should take her own life, or have it taken for her, or have anyone permit that it be taken. (This attitude may, as I have argued, be felt by the woman herself, or any of the other characters in the story, as a personal religious conviction, a matter of faith; but it may also be a settled and publicly stated principle, among those who have come to be called Pro-Lifers whether or not they are religious believers.) The issue of the sanctity of human life must be faced; but it comes up in perhaps a more acute form in our second story, to which we may therefore now turn.

The main differences between our first and our second story are these: in the second story the girl is not suffering; she does not wish to die (nor, for that matter, does she wish not to die: she is beyond having wishes of any kind); she is not terminally ill. She reached the position she is in through an accident, and immediate medical intervention took place to save her life, after which arrangements were made to feed her artificially. If nature had been allowed to take its course she would have died as an immediate result of the accident; and thereafter, even if she had been alive for a time, she would have died because she could take neither food nor water. But no one would have thought it right not to try to save her, and having saved her, no one would have thought it right not to arrange for nutrition and hydration to be given artificially. For at that stage no one knew whether she would recover or not. But the result is that now 'letting nature take its course', that is letting her die of an infection or of old age, means continuing with her artificial nutrition and hydration. The only way she could now die as she would have died without the artificial feeding is to withdraw that feeding. The concept of the natural is even more confusing in this case than in the first.

This leads directly to a preliminary point. In the story, the Law Lords finally ruled that the girl be allowed to die, that is to die 'naturally', of starvation and dehydration. They did not allow that the doctor give her a lethal injection. They were therefore relying on a distinction between killing and allowing to die. If the doctor had been permitted to administer a lethal injection he would have been thus permitted to commit murder, which is deliberately and intentionally to cause the death of another person, with whatever motive.

There are areas in the law where the distinction between killing and letting die is a valid one, I have no doubt. If I, a competent swimmer with a life-saving certificate, am walking by the canal, and see you in the water, unable to swim, and sinking fast, I will not be charged with murder if I do not jump in and rescue you. I shall doubtless, when the story comes out, be greatly blamed, and my moral character will be ruined. But I have not deliberately taken your life, as I would have if I had pushed you into the canal in the first place. I have, however, undoubtedly let you die. But in the situation described in our second story, I do not believe that the distinction has any validity, nor, certainly, any ethical relevance. It rests on a primitive notion of cause, that a cause must always be an action, a pushing or pulling, a kicking or jabbing with a needle. And of course these actions are the most perceptible causes that there are. I can feel the push which sends me hurtling down the stairs; I can see and hear the bat striking the ball which crashes through the greenhouse roof. But in real life we know that there are other causes. I can kill my pet by neglect as well as by running her over; the storming of a fortress may be caused by the sentry's failure to come on duty as well as by a battering ram. There seems to be no difference in the responsibility to be allocated in the two kinds of cases. Indeed morally speaking it would usually be less cruel to give a lethal injection than to allow a patient to die of thirst and starvation. (In our story that question did not arise, since the patient was incapable of experiencing anything; and that included the pangs of hunger and thirst.) But, as a general rule, I can see no ethical difference between deliberately killing and deliberately letting die, though the former may avoid the extra charge of cruelty.

In the second story, everyone who had been fond of the girl wanted her to die, one way or another. It was the hospital which disallowed her death until they had the ruling of the judiciary. They are likely to have been under pressure not only from those who thought that the death would be legally unsafe, but also from those who thought it would be morally wrong. So once again we must examine the issues. Those who wanted her to die, her family and friends, wanted this not because of her sufferings, which she did not experience, but, quite simply, because they judged that her life was not worth living. Not being in pain is not the only thing that gives life value; activity, perception, intelligence and enjoyment are equally important values; and her life contained none of these things. Their own sufferings in seeing her every day, and of hope finally extinguished, must have been acute, and seen to be so by everyone who knew them, even if they themselves did not adduce this as a reason for ending her life. But they must, very properly, have longed for this pseudo-life to be ended, so that they could place the terrible story of their daughter or girlfriend in their own annals of suffering, as genuinely belonging to a remembered past. It seems that no one could dissent from these feelings, at the level of private moral sentiment.

The dissentient voices come, then, on the whole not from the private but the public arena. However, there is one argument that may be used in our second story which may be felt equally as a matter of private conscience and of public policy. It is an argument focused on the name of the patient's condition, 'Permanent Vegetative State'. For how can it be certainly known to be permanent? One is always hearing stories of amazing recoveries from coma, even from a state that has been diagnosed with confidence as permanently vegetative. Must not the relatives of the girl in the story feel bound to have her kept alive, simply in the hope that she has been misdiagnosed, and that she will one day come to life? If they press on with their requests that she be released from her non-life, will they not always have the lurking fear that she might after all have recovered if she had been given time? Equally the hospital might argue that it would be an appallingly un-ethical decision to allow this patient to die, if some other doctors somewhere else might produce evidence that her state was not, or not necessarily, permanent, and this might be the basis of their hesitation, and their under-standable wish to have themselves covered by the law.

This anxiety seems to me reasonable and inevitable, up to a point. It certainly provides an argument for leaving the girl alive for a longish time after her accident. But it is, I believe, a problem which demands a medical solution. There should be strict and agreed criteria for what counts as PVS, and these should be derived as far as possible from evidence as to the physiological state of the brain of the patient, not from her symptoms. If this evidence sug-gests either that she cannot recover, or that, even if she recovered a little, the damage to her brain would still be devastating, and her life of hopelessly low quality, then PVS should be the diagnosis, and the ending of her life ethically acceptable, if that is what her family want. Nev-ertheless the fear of misdiagnosis must be taken very seriously, for it is certain to be an additional source of suffering for her relatives after she is dead. There should always be at least two doctors to concur with the diagno-sis; and the family will not be wholly reassured unless they thoroughly trust the doctors.

We can turn now to matters of ethical policy, to the sphere, that is, of public morality. In hearing evidence about a case like that in our second story, the House of Lords Select Committee listened to, and took part in, one argument which I think can be got out of the way at the beginning. This was an argument put forward by nurses, that, though they would not have objected to switching off a life-support machine in certain circumstances (and if the family so wished), the withdrawal of artificial nutrition and hydration was ethically an altogether different matter. I report this argument, but I find it impossible to sympathise with it. The argument seemed to be that where someone needed help to breathe, or to keep her heart beating (which the girl in our story did not), then this was a medical treatment, and it could be deemed by doctors that the treatment was futile and could therefore legitimately be withdrawn. To eat and drink, on the other hand, is not to receive treatment, by whatever artificial devices the processes are brought about. A nurse, it was claimed, has as an absolute minimum duty to supply food and drink to patients, and this apart from any treatment that the doctors in charge may deem suitable. Therefore they could not countenance the withdrawal of the necessary tubes, though presumably they might have had no objection to the administering of a lethal injection, while the tubes were still attached. A great deal of scholastic discussion has gone on as to what counts as 'treatment', what counts as 'artificial' as opposed to 'natural' feeding, and whether there is an ethical difference between a kind of drip system for feeding, which could be used only in a hospital setting (which might qualify it to count as 'treatment') and, say, a teaspoon or a specially designed cup, by means of which you could deliver soup into the mouth of a patient unable to feed herself at home. But it seems obvious that, just as doctors *usually* have a duty to treat patients who are ill, so *usually* nurses have a duty to supervise their nutrition and hydration; but that either of these duties may be overridden if, for other reasons, it seems best that the patient should die. I for one can see no difference in status between these two sets of duties. There was no more reason why the nurses should obstinately persist in carrying out their duties, if these were futile, than that the doctors should. It may sound marginally worse to say that someone was deprived of food and drink than that they were deprived of treatment; but this is, in the given circumstances, a sentimental distinction, based on tradition, not one of ethical significance. The nurses were relying on a feeling about their duty, but it was not a moral feeling insofar as it was based, not on a consideration of the whole of the situation, but only on their own part in it.

We are left, then, with the other arguments in the sphere of public morality, the field of policy as distinct from private conscience. These arguments are difficult to separate one from another. It will be seen that they fuse together. First, there is the argument we have already partly examined, that all human life is sacred, and no life must be deliberately brought to an end. To choose that a

patient die rather than continue to live is frequently referred to as an instance of a doctor's playing God (though
in this case, as in our first story, the play-acting would
have been carried out with the full approval of the relatives of the patient).

Looking at this argument again, in the context of the
second story, it seems that to speak of human life as sacred
may be a shorthand way of speaking about God and His
creation, but it may also, and perhaps in a secular age
more frequently, conceal a thoroughly secular fear. That
this is perhaps more obvious in the second story than in
the first, is explained by the fact that the woman in the first
story was terminally ill; and unless this had been so, the
doctor quite certainly would not have hastened her death
by the administering of extra morphia. In the second story,
on the contrary, the patient is not terminally ill. There is
no foreseeable end to her natural life, if such it can be
called. To declare that human life is sacred is to declare it
inviolable; it must not be deliberately taken, though the
heavens fall. And the determination to uphold this value
is strong, in the context of the second story, just because
of the fear that if the life of the girl with PVS is deemed
expendable, though left, as it were, to herself she might
live for many years, then other lives might become expendable too, lives of those with less catastrophic but
nevertheless incurable conditions such as severe brain
damage of various different sorts, or progressive illnesses
where the patient might all the same have many years of
life ahead. The scope of the doctor's decision is not

limited in the way that it is in the first story, where it is limited to those who are soon to die anyway, and the question is simply how they die, in anguish or otherwise. The inviolability or sanctity of human life must be reasserted, in the second story, because of the apparent open-ended nature of the final decision of the judges, that the life of the girl was not worth preserving.

What we have here is a version of the 'slippery slope' argument. This argument has a great power over the imagination. Though there may be no great ethical objection to the deliberate ending of the life of the girl in our second story, the question is raised Where will it end? Once embarked on the slope, what is to prevent our slithering down through various apparently not dissimilar cases, to an ethical quagmire at the bottom of the slope, where we shall countenance the killing off of any people who are both helpless and expensive to maintain? Very often at this stage in the presentation of the argument, mention is made of Nazi Germany, and the deliberate killing-off of Jews. But this is an unnecessary and confusing step to take, and it is usually taken more for rhetorical effect than for the sake of logic. For it is easy to distinguish even widespread euthanasia as described in our second story from the racially-inspired behaviour of the Nazis. To decide that Jews are expendable, or rather that they deserve no better than to die, is of a different order from deciding that some genuinely incurable patients are living a life of such low quality that they are better dead, though innocent of any offence. But, leaving aside any reference to Nazis and Jews, the slippery slope is nevertheless an argument that has to be addressed.

Of course the slippery slope argument is not strictly a *logical* argument at all. There is no *logical* connection between allowing a PVS patient to die and allowing the death of other patients who are afflicted in quite different ways. It is an argument about human nature: give them an inch, and they'll take an ell. It is, in this case, essentially an argument to be used by people who do not trust doctors or hospital ethics committees. There may be the fear, too, that hospitals, whatever words they may use about further treatment not being 'appropriate', are really talking about resources. And though my own view is that it is perfectly reasonable to take into account the expense of keeping alive a PVS patient, whether by the expenditure of private or public money, in coming to a decision about continuing her life, yet people are always afraid that such considerations are weighing unduly with the doctor or the hospital, though unavowed.

So we end with the question whether there is any way to block the descent down the slope, in a manner that people can trust. I have no doubt whatever that the death of the patients in the two stories was morally right (though I think it would have been morally better to give the patient in the second story a lethal injection. In fact no harm was done to her by allowing her to starve to death, since she was already beyond harm; but it must have been emotionally upsetting for the nurses who had looked after her for so long to stand by, now, and wait for her to die;

and the same must be true of the parents). Because of the particular circumstances surrounding each of the women in our stories, the value of their death was greater than the value of their continued life. In both cases it was the value, or quality, of their lives that had to be assessed. In the first story, the woman herself had a part, the greatest part, in determining what was the quality of her own life, and she judged that its quality was exceptionally low, as was that of her husband's life, as long as she lived on. Unless it is held that all human life is 'sacred' in one of the senses considered already, one must conclude that life itself is not intrinsically valuable. Its value depends on what it is like, its quality. And on this basis the value judgement was arrived at. In the second story the quality of the life of the girl could scarcely have been lower, though she could have no share in judging this for herself. In the first story, the doctor judged, as I have argued, that it was more important, or mattered more morally, to end his patient's distress than to continue with her poor-quality life. In the second story, while no such obvious trade-off was possible, it could be said that it mattered more morally to accede to the wishes of the relatives, and end their misery, than it did to keep the patient alive, when there was nothing good for her in living as she was. Could one block the slippery slope by generalising these particular circumstances, and taking them as the unique circumstances in which a patient's life might be ended? For a good way to prevent a descent down a slippery slope is to introduce legislation which, in effect, says, 'You may go so far and no further' on pain of criminal prosecution. So the slippery slope could be rendered safe by changing legislation and legalising euthanasia in cases such as those in our two stories, or, more reassuringly, ruling that euthanasia is illegal, except in cases such as these. But the objection to that (and I regard it as a fatal or at any rate a virtually insuperable objection) lies in the words 'such as'. If the law were more precise (let us say it had lists of conditions where euthanasia might legally be practised), then there would inevitably arise hard cases, or cases not envisaged by the law. Such specificity is hardly ever suitable to be included in an Act of Parliament. On the other hand the imprecision of 'such as', if contained in the Act, would lead to endless disputes about whether a particular case had been within the law or not.

Attitudes may change. It is possible to imagine a law, rather like the law governing abortion, whereby certain specific requirements were laid down for legalised voluntary euthanasia. This would perhaps crystallise in law what is coming to seem a more and more acceptable ending to our first story. If, short of legislation, this still involves doctors in the game-playing of the argument from double effect, then this is a small price to pay for what is really an exercise on their part of a compassionate value judgement about what is and what is not tolerable. And they do not make this judgement by themselves. They have the support of the patient herself and her husband, in our story, and in many similar stories. There is, however, no let-out by means of double effect, in the second story. The doctor intends to kill the patient, or let her die, and he has no intention short of this. There is no other possible reason to order the feeding-tubes to be removed. Here it seems to me there is nothing to be done except to examine each case before it comes to the point of decision, at the moment, say, when PVS has been carefully and scrupulously diagnosed. Then perhaps the hospital ethics committee (for these will all be hospital cases) may risk a decision, acting on the precedent of stories like our second story; or they may at once seek a judicial review. It is sometimes held that it should not be lawyers but doctors who make decisions of life or death. I disagree. Lawyers can act, after all, on medical evidence. And it must certainly be lawyers who decide whether, in all the circumstances of the case, murder has been committed. Murder is a concept that is both legal and moral. But because of the closeness of legal and moral in this context, the decision whether to kill the patient *would be* murder in such a case is a question raised essentially as a matter of *public* morality, which is to say, as a matter of law.

Birth

If I spend rather less time on questions surrounding birth than I spent on death, it is because a number of the questions, for example whether human life has an intrinsic value, independent of what kind of life it is, how long or short its duration, have already been raised, in the previous chapter. But they have not been wholly answered, nor even fully enough discussed, for a respectable guide through the quagmire we are about to descend into, as we face questions about assisted births and in vitro fertilisation, and the ethics of research using human embryos, as well as about abortion. In the consideration of these matters, the inter-relation between private moral convictions and public policy turns out to be exceedingly complex.

The ethical questions raised in the first-mentioned area differ in one important respect from those raised about euthanasia. People have always died, and there is no doubt that doctors have always ministered to the comfort of the dying in whatever ways were available to them. In contrast, the moral questions that have arisen about assisted reproduction are new. There were no such questions thirty years ago; and only twenty years ago the first embryos fertilised in the laboratory were beginning to come into being. It is about the status to be accorded to such embryos that the crucial moral questions arise. It was on account of the novelty of the problems that, in the late 1970s, it seemed clear that legislation was called for, to regulate the new research, and to reassure the public that we were not entering an era of totally uncontrolled manipulation of the future of the human race. There were no precedents here that could help, and no received wisdom.

Questions about the ethics of infertility treatments entered my life abruptly when, in 1982, I was asked to chair a Government Committee of Enquiry into Human Fertilisation and Embryology. The committee was set up as a result of increasing public awareness of (and to some extent unease about) the new techniques involved in assisted reproduction, following the birth in 1978 of the first 'test-tube baby', or baby born by in vitro fertilisation. It was a world-first, and took place in Stockport, near Manchester. The technique involves the collection of sperm from the male partner of an infertile couple, and of eggs from the female partner, and their fertilisation in a dish (or test-tube) in the laboratory, in a medium simulating, as far as possible, the natural medium within which fertilisation takes place in the female body. If and when fertilisation has been achieved in the 'test-tube' the resulting embryo, or embryos, is placed in the uterus of the woman, and will, with luck, implant in the wall of the uterus, after which a normal pregnancy will follow. This treatment was at first thought suitable almost exclusively for women who had defective fallopian tubes, up which sperm could not travel; but later it was thought that it might be useful also where a man had a low sperm count, and controlled laboratory conditions were more likely to lead to successful fertilisation than ordinary methods.

The techniques of in vitro fertilisation are now widely accepted as more or less routine (though the success rate is not enormously high, even today). However, at the beginning there were those who objected to the use of the techniques themselves, as 'unnatural'; but this argument is no more secure than any other argument based on the concept of the natural. So at least it seemed to the committee, and so it seems to me.

There were also a few who objected to the use of public funds for any infertility treatment or research, in a world suffering from over-population. The committee did not take this objection very seriously. Compared with the number of births worldwide, the number of births by any kind of assisted reproduction was, and would remain, minute. Besides, we argued that infertility is a physical malfunction which can cause immense distress to individuals, and therefore the medical profession was ethically entitled, indeed bound, to seek ways to remedy the malfunction when appealed to by couples wanting to conceive.

The abiding moral objection to the use of in vitro fertilisation, however, is its reliance on continued research using live human embryos. For if in vitro fertilisation is to continue to be offered to infertile patients, its success rate has to be improved; and this cannot be done without continuing laboratory research into the best environment in which to achieve fertilisation outside the body. This inevitably entails that human embryos must be used experimentally and then destroyed. More-over, since the 1980s, other scientific research involving the use of embryos has become even more important. There is much still to be learned about the process of fertilisation itself, and about the development of the cells of the very newly fertilised embryo. Such research has widened the field within which live embryos must be used. The increase in knowledge so gained promises medical advances such as the possible identification and replacement of faulty genes, which in turn might lead to treatment of many devastating and hitherto untreatable mono-genetic diseases. Indeed by the time the Embryol-ogy Bill came to be debated in Parliament in 1989 and 1990, the emphasis in the discussion of research using human embryos had shifted substantially from infertility treatment to questions concerned with genetic diseases. It is against this background of possible profound changes in medical practice that the discussion of the ethics of embryo research must be seen.

Here, then, appears to me the central ethical problem: to what extent is it morally permissible to use live em-bryos as research material? These embryos are *ex hypothesi* both human and alive. To what extent may they be treated as different from other human beings? For no grown-up human may be used for research without con-sent, and no child may be so used, even with the consent of his or her parents. And if these other humans may not be used for research, still less may they thereafter be destroyed.

I will first outline the conclusion the Committee of Enquiry came to (by a majority), now enshrined in legislation, and then go back over the moral issues involved. As the law now stands, it is permissible, subject to the licensing of each research project by a statutory body, the Human Fertility and Embryology Authority, to use a human embryo for research for up to fourteen days from fertilisation in the laboratory, and then to destroy it. Maintaining an embryo alive, unfrozen, for longer than fourteen days is a criminal offence, with penalties of up to ten years' imprisonment attached. The law thus deems that the embryo undergoes a dramatic change of status after fourteen days from fertilisation (not counting as relevant any days during which the embryo is frozen), thereafter being protected from use as a research-object almost as rigorously as a child is protected.

We, the Committee of Enquiry, recommended this change of status at fourteen days because of the physiological changes in the embryo at that time. Before fourteen days from fertilisation, we argued, the embryo is not really one thing, but a loose collection of cells that have not yet differentiated (often referred to as the pre-embryo). Any one of these cells may take on any role when the embryo forms, or may become part of the placenta, rather than of the embryo itself. The cells are totipotent. Moreover for up to fourteen days it is possible that twinning will take place, and that there will, if normal development occurs, be two individuals who are born, rather than one. It is therefore difficult for me, or anyone else, to trace my origin as an individual back beyond the fourteen-day stage to the stage when I might have been two. Who, which of the two, would 'I' be? At about fourteen days, however, what is known as the 'primitive streak' appears, which is a piling up of cells, as they reproduce themselves, at the caudal end of the embryonic disc; and this is the first beginning of what will become the spinal cord and central nervous system of the embryo. From this moment on, the embryo as a whole grows and develops extremely rapidly, and the cells are differentiated into their future functions. The committee therefore argued that there was a morally significant difference between the pre- and post-fourteen-day cells, in that only after fourteen days can the human individual properly be said to exist. And it is the human individual who must not be used for research and then destroyed.

It is sometimes argued against this that the individual human must exist before the appearance of the primitive streak, because all of the genome, the complete set of the hereditary factors of the embryo, is already in place from fertilisation onwards. But this argument suggests that an individual human is nothing except his genome. This cannot be true. For one thing, the whole genetic make-up of a person can be discovered from a small bit of tissue, or a drop of saliva; yet we do not think of these as *being* the person. Moreover it is his whole developing body and brain which distinguishes him from other individuals. Even identical twins, whose genome is shared, develop differently from one another at the level of the functioning and thus the development of their brains. It is perfectly consistent, therefore, to hold that though the genetic factors in an individual's development may be given at the zygote stage (that is the one-cell stage immediately following fertilisation of egg and sperm), the individual himself has not yet come into being.

There was, and is, an enormous difficulty in discussing the ethical issues here involved. There is a strong tendency for people on both sides of the ethical debate, but especially for those opposed to any research using human embryos, to raise the question When does human life begin? But even those who raise this question most insistently, and who tend to answer it by saying that human life begins at 'the moment of fertilisation' (though in fact fertilisation is a process, not an event), know that in a way the question is misleading. For they are perfectly well aware that the gametes, sperm and egg, are human (they do not belong to any other species) and are alive. As far as biological life goes, they know that new life does not spring into existence when the gametes come together to form the zygote, the new cell. Life has been there before. What they are really asking, as I have just suggested, is when a new human individual should be thought to begin to exist.

And here there remain in many people's minds the vestiges of another, much older question, namely, when does 'ensoulment' occur? We must go back to Aristotle, whose theories of the early development of life had a vast influence on later thinking, especially, through Aquinas, on the thinking of the Roman Catholic Church (though Aquinas's teaching was by no mean immediately accepted by the Church). Aristotle held that there was a straight scientific answer to the question of the development in the fetus of different kinds of soul, or life.[*] According to his view, the soul was the life appropriate to different stages of development of any living thing, plant or animal. There were three kinds of life: vegetable, that which was alone appropriate to plants; a kind of life capable of sensation and perception, which belongs to all animals; and the kind of life unique to humans, the rational life. In the development of the human fetus, Aristotle held that each of these kinds of life enters at a different stage of the pregnancy. When the embryo is first formed it has only vegetable life, then it acquires animal life, and is capable of sensation, and finally, at forty days from conception in the case of men and ninety in the case of women, the fetus acquires rational or mental life. This was a perfectly sensible biological theory, based, as it necessarily was, on guesswork. (One must not forget the vast difference made to our knowledge of obstetrics by the invention of the microscope. Aristotle did not even know of the existence of the ovum.) Aquinas, who died in 1274, revived Aristotle's philosophy, virtually unknown since antiquity, and among many other things took over almost

* Aristotle *de partibus animalium* and *de anima*.

word for word his account of the development of the embryo. Thus he held that the soul enters the forming embryo by stages, first the vegetable, then the perceptive and finally the rational, each aspect of the soul taking over and embracing the one before until, after forty days or ninety, depending on gender, conception was complete. But of course the new Aristotelianism of Aquinas was based on a different, non-biological, and specifically religious idea of the soul, as that which is immortal and is saved by faith. So, though the question When does life begin? may look like a rather carelessly phrased Aristotelian question, to be answered empirically, as Aristotle tried to answer it, yet in the context of Christianity it becomes a question charged with religious significance. The life or soul, according to Christian tradition, is that which enters a temporary union with the flesh, appearing at birth, and surviving death. It is that which alone has value.

It is this half-remembered, seldom articulated baggage that the question When does life begin? carries with it. There is, among those who raise the question in this form, an inevitable ambiguity as to whether they are speaking of life as simply biological life, or as something specifically human, that which belongs to, is lived by, each individual human being, each of whom has value in his own right.

It would therefore be much clearer and less misleading if people asked at what stage an embryo becomes morally significant; or at what stage we ought to start to treat a human embryo as we treat other human beings. It would then be clear that no further scientific knowledge would settle the question. It is a matter of ethical decision, a decision that society had to make in the period of consultation before the Embryology Act was passed, and Parliament had to make during the passage of the Bill. During the passage of the Bill there was no party whip involved. Each member of both Houses voted freely according to conscience. For what is at issue, as I have said, is the moral status to be accorded to the very early embryo in the laboratory. There are no analogies to help us here, and it is of no use to scan Holy Writ for an answer. Until a few years earlier there had been no such entities as separate four- or sixteen-cell embryos, existing outside the body. The question was new. Of course the science of embryonic development had a bearing on the moral decision that had to be taken; no one can make a sound moral judgement without knowledge of the facts about which they are to judge. And a close scrutiny of the facts may seem almost necessarily to dictate a moral judgement. Thus, in my own case, and that of a majority in both Houses, the very fact of the development of the primitive streak, the true emergence of one single individual, on however physically tiny a scale, seemed to dictate the judgement that one could treat the collection of cells before this stage differently from its treatment thereafter, and that, given the immense benefits that will come from research using these very early embryos, or pre-embryos, it was right that they should be used.

It is because of the vestigial presence of an Aristotelian and Thomist belief about the soul's entry into the body at a specific moment that moral, biological and religious issues are prone to become so inextricably tangled in this case. The presupposition of the present law is completely different: the embryo develops gradually from the beginning of the process of fertilisation, and it is for us to value the emerging life as we think right, according to its development. The then Archbishop of York, John Habgood, put this very clearly, in defending the fourteen-day cut-off point for the use of embryos for research (*Hansard*, 7th December 1989): 'Scientists in general and biologists in particular deal mostly in continuities and in gradual changes from one state to another. This is true of evolution, in which the transition from the pre-human to the human took place over countless generations. There was never a precise moment when it could have been said, "Here is a hominid and here is a man." But this is not to deny that as a result of the process there emerged a profound and indeed crucial set of differences between hominids and men. The same is true of individual lives … It seems strange to a biologist that all the weight of moral argument should be placed on one definable moment at the beginning. What matters is the process.' And he went on to say, to the alarm of some, 'Christians are no more required to believe that humanness is created in an instant than we are required to believe in the historical existence of Adam and Eve.' (This led at a later stage of the debate, when someone remarked that no Christian could countenance research using early embryos, and it was pointed out that the Archbishop had argued in favour of it, to the reply that it was well known that the Archbishop was not a Christian.)

There were other ethical issues that had to be addressed by the Committee of Enquiry, such as the proper regulation of artificial insemination by donor, and the moral status of surrogacy, especially surrogacy organised as a commercial business, which was then beginning to be introduced into the UK from the United States. But none, in my opinion, raised such fundamental moral questions as the issue of research using human embryos. For this was genuinely a matter of life and death; of the sanctity or expendability of human life.

There were, of course, those who, as in the case of euthanasia, were wholly opposed to the use of human embryos for research, and their subsequent destruction, whatever the benefits might be in terms of the consequences, whether for particular infertile couples or for the general advance of knowledge. These people relied on an absolute doctrine, that no one must deliberately take a human life, at whatever stage of development.

Such absolutists were not interested in hearing about the medical advances that might arise out of research, nor about the relief to infertile couples. They were simply opposed in principle to the deliberate taking of human life, whether the embryos used had been specially brought into being for the purposes of research, or whether they were 'spare' embryos, left over from the collecting of eggs from a woman seeking IVF treatment, after as many eggs as seemed medically best had been placed in the uterus. If any embryos were used for research, they argued, then these must themselves be placed in a woman's uterus, so that they might have a chance of life. But this practice was never upheld as morally tolerable by doctors, since they could not know to what damage embryos used for research had been subjected, and to place them in the uterus of a woman would be to use her as an experimental subject, at a time when, hoping desperately for a healthy child, she was at her most vulnerable.

In addition, as in the euthanasia debate, the slippery slope argument was widely deployed. (And indeed many of those wholly opposed to research used this argument as a kind of back-up, though logically they should not have. For their position was that one should never have got on to the slope in the first place.) It was in this connection that I learned how powerful a weapon the law could be in definitively blocking the slope, so that we might not be at risk of slithering down to the bottom. This was the function of the fourteen-day limit on research. Cynics said that I was hopelessly naive to think that this law would work to block the descent down the slope. But, as far as I know, no one has attempted to keep an embryo alive in the laboratory for longer than the permitted fourteen days; and the laboratory inspectorate, set up under the statutory authority, has worked effectively. However, there is no doubt that there *could* be rogue laboratories where embryos were being kept alive longer, contrary to the law. The reason why I think this unlikely is not only because of the sanctions that would be imposed by the law if these scientists were discovered (say by trying to publish their research findings), but because in this case the criminal law followed closely what appeared to be the moral consensus of those, in Parliament and outside, who were concerned with the issues. That is to say, the distinction between the embryo up to fourteen days from fertilisation and the embryo thereafter seemed to those concerned to be a genuinely morally significant distinction. The slope was not blocked arbitrarily at a particular point, but in accordance with a moral barrier that people did not want to cross. It is largely because it is so difficult to think of an equally simple block on the slippery slope in the case of euthanasia that I am opposed to any attempt to change the law, to render some kinds of euthanasia legitimate.

I learned something else about the relation between public and private morality from this debate and its outcome. As a general rule, legislation must be broadly utilitarian in outlook. That is to say a party or a government hoping to introduce new legislation about, let us say, emissions of noxious fumes into the environment, the disposal of nuclear waste, or the redistribution of wavelengths among radio companies, must primarily have regard to the weight of benefits over harms to people at large. Such calculations are extremely difficult to carry out, and there may be numerous vested interests involved which make a simple counting of heads useless, even if it were possible. Nevertheless broadly speaking, in trying to decide what it would be best to do, legislators must be consequentialists. They must foresee as far as they can who will benefit from the new law, and who will suffer, and to what extent. In such calculations, each member of society should count for one, and no one should be given special consideration. This is the ideal, however far from achieving it particular governments may be (for all are subject to the lobbying of special interest groups). However, in the case of the decision whether or not to permit research using human embryos, no such utilitarian calculation was possible. It could be argued, and was argued by some, that the benefits to individual infertile couples, and to society at large, through new medical knowledge, were vast, and there was no one who was harmed. Therefore everything was on the side of research being permitted. But, though it was true that no existing people were harmed by the research, the embryos themselves who were the subjects of research suffered what would usually be thought the greatest harm possible, namely they were destroyed. The whole question at issue was thus whether or not very early embryos counted or did not count in the calculus of benefits and harms. John Stuart Mill, whose *Utilitarianism* (1851) is one of the classic texts of this kind of consequentialist moral philosophy, said (without arguing it) that 'children and savages' did not count in the calculus of benefits and harms. He would certainly have ruled out embryos, if he ruled out children. But no purely utilitarian argument could serve to settle the question of who *should* count. The central question, What status should be accorded to the early embryo?, had to be settled by different means. And the only means available was the degree to which people felt that the early embryo was in fact, to all intents and purposes, a child. For, as I have suggested, no one would countenance the use of children for research, still less their subsequent destruction. As it turned out, a majority felt that the early embryo, before it had formed itself into a single individual and (having as yet no central nervous system) before it was capable of even rudimentary sensation or perception, was not sufficiently like a child to be accorded the status of a child. Therefore research was permitted. Utilitarian considerations came in, insofar as the benefits to the infertile and to society at large were cited in justification of research. The consequences to the embryos were discounted.

What I learned from these arguments and their outcome was that there is a difference between what is a generally agreed moral view (as, for instance, that children should not be used as subjects of research) and a morality which, though not agreed, is nevertheless broadly *acceptable*. When I first came across the use of the word 'acceptable' in this kind of context, I thought of it as a typical civil service cop-out. It was, I thought, mealy-mouthed. They, the civil servants, did not want to use strong and definite words which would commit them, words like 'right' and 'wrong'. But I came to see that I was here confusing private with public morality. In public issues where there is a radical difference of moral opinion (as between those who think the early embryo should have the same moral status as a child and those who do not), and where no compromise is possible, the concept of the acceptable is a useful and indeed indispensable one. Although the legislation which emerged from these particular debates could not satisfy those who held that all human life was sacred, yet at least by blocking the slippery slope, the legislation limited the damage, and did satisfy both those who whole-heartedly advocated research, and those who relied on the slippery slope argument alone to object to it. The outcome became one that people could live with, even though they were of course entitled both to refuse individually to have anything to do with in vitro fertilisation, and to continue to form pressure groups to try to get the legislation changed. Thus, as far as public morality goes, the concept of the acceptable is necessary, in that it may set the best goal possible in the circumstances.

It has often been remarked that the embryology law, which offers protection to embryos over fourteen days from fertilisation, stands in stark contrast with the laws governing abortion, where fetuses may, in certain circumstances, be destroyed when they are as much as twenty-eight weeks in gestational age, and where there are no restrictions on using fetuses for research purposes (though of course such fetuses would not be alive at the time). The two laws are, however, radically different in their intention, and the moral considerations that lie behind them are also different. The only thing they have in common is that both fall foul of those who hold that human life is sacred and must be preserved from the 'moment' of fertilisation onwards to death.

The first difference to notice is in the circumstances in which legislation arose. In the wholly new consideration of the status of the embryo alive in the laboratory, it was open to Government to decide to prohibit all research, and lay down, as some wished, that any embryo brought into existence in a 'test-tube' must be placed in a woman's uterus. This would have been, in effect, to prohibit in vitro fertilisation itself. It would have been to use the woman as an experimental object, and even if there were women who were so desperate to bear a child that they would have permitted this, no reputable doctor would treat a woman in these circumstances. It was possible, however, that Government might have been prepared to bring all in vitro fertilisation treatment to an end. In the case of abortion, on the other hand, there was and is no possibility of putting a stop to it altogether, whatever those who are opposed to it may wish. For years abortion was a crime, but it took place none the less, and with disastrous consequences in terms of deaths from back-street abortions. There was an overwhelming case for regulating rather than prohibiting abortion, and this is what legislation set out to do. Even those who regard abortion as murder recognise the fact that criminalising it again is not a real option in a world where most people do not regard it in this light. Once again, all that absolutists can do is refuse to have anything to do with abortion, whether for themselves or for their patients, if they are doctors. But even in the latter case, they on the whole recognise that since abortion is not any longer a crime, they have a duty to help their patients to have access to a doctor who will legitimately carry it out, if these patients are certain that they have good reason to seek an abortion.

The view that abortion is murder turns, as I have said, on the view that a fetus is a human individual (often referred to as a 'person') who must not be killed. I shall return to the concept of a 'person' in the following chapter. For the time, it should be noted that there is a presumption in law that abortion simply on demand, and because the mother or the couple want it, for whatever reason, would be wrong, and that therefore certain criteria have to be satisfied if an abortion is to be carried out legally. That is to say it is presumed that there is something wrong with aborting a fetus, even if what is wrong with doing so is not the same as what is wrong with murdering someone. Moreover, among those who do not wholly reject legitimate abortion, there is a strong belief that an early abortion, say within the first twelve weeks of a pregnancy, is to be preferred to a late abortion. This is of course partly a pragmatic matter: an early abortion is easier and safer to carry out. But there is also a generally held feeling that, even if it can be managed safely, a late abortion, carried out when the fetus is almost fully formed, and after the pregnancy has lasted so long that the fetus might be capable of being born alive (say at twenty-three or twenty-four weeks), is more like infanticide than abortion, and thus more like murder. There is no doubt that such an abortion is traumatic for all those concerned in it, including doctors and nurses. Those pro-life campaigners who regard *all* abortion as murder ought not, in principle, to make any distinction between early and late abortions. Yet it is plain that they, like other people, often do. There seems to be thus some confirmation of the gradualist or developmental view of the status we accord to human embryos and fetuses. The further along the path towards being born a fetus has progressed, the more protection we feel it should have from being destroyed, and the more urgent the reason for an abortion needs to be (for example that the life of the mother is at stake). And the law recognises this. Late abortions cannot be undertaken frivolously; they may be carried out only in National Health Service hospitals, not in private clinics or nursing homes; and, as things are, only a very few are in fact carried out every year.

In the case of very early embryos, the fourteen-day cut-off point, after which an embryo may not be kept alive in the laboratory, serves as a marker for a change in the moral status of the embryo. It would be highly satisfactory if some analogous cut-off point could be found, a physiological watershed which would allow abortion on demand, without guilt or moral disapproval, up to and not beyond a specific point in the pregnancy, after which the kinds of regulation currently imposed on all abortions should begin to operate. Many European countries in fact allow abortion more or less on demand up to twelve weeks of pregnancy, and this may be a satisfactory solution, even if lacking the physiological definiteness of the emergence of the primitive streak. As things are, in the UK, those of us who do not hold an absolute or abolitionist view of abortion seem ambivalent in our attitude. Abortion is not a crime, to carry out an abortion is not murder; but what is it? We seem to be saying that abortion is a pity; it is something that needs justification in a way that, in most people's eyes, contraception, even 'morning-after' contraception, does not. Most people are quite capable of separating the sexual act from what once was thought of as the natural, almost inevitable, consequence of that act, namely the conception of a child. Thus the use of contraceptives has come to seem not only acceptable, but often a matter of duty. But if we follow the logic of the argument which distinguished the pre-embryo from the embryo, or the pre- from the post-fourteen-day embryo, then we can have no doubt that abortion is the destruction of an individual human being, and it is this that makes us uneasy.

Nevertheless, both at the level of public morality, or social policy, and, often, at the level of the private morality concerned with individual cases, it is broadly utilitarian considerations that are most powerful, for non-absolutists. At the public level, as I have argued, abortion is and will remain something which occurs. The policy aim must be to see that it occurs in as little damaging a way as possible, and governed by regulation that will be 'acceptable' (though here, as elsewhere, we have to remember that the 'acceptable' is a matter of balance, and it may change from time to time). At the level of individual decision about abortion, it seems to me that we judge each case separately; and often can have no doubt that abortion is the best, it may seem the only tolerable, solution to the problems caused by an unwanted pregnancy. In my days as a headmistress, I more than once encouraged a sixteen- or seventeen-year-old girl to have an abortion, as quickly as possible, and come back to get on with her A-levels. I did not regret these decisions, nor did the girls in question, who had no desire whatever to have the child of the person who had, if not raped, then at least casually seduced them. In another different kind of case a girl of sixteen came to see me with a beaming smile to tell me that, by accident, she was pregnant, and wasn't it wonderful? Now she could leave school. (And she came back to visit the school later, still delighted, with the baby in a pram, and its equally delighted grandmother at her side.) Circumstances differ. I am thankful that abortion is no longer a crime. But there still seems to me to be a shifty ambivalence, a sort of moral mist, hanging in the air.

It is perhaps in an attempt to clear away this mist that it has become almost universal to discuss questions about abortion in terms of rights: the right of the mother to determine what shall go on in her own body; or the right of the fetus to be born, and have its own life. In the following chapter I shall consider the implications of a rights-based morality, both in connection with abortion, and more widely.

Rights

The discussions of life and death in the foregoing chapters might all have been couched in terms of rights: the right of a terminally ill patient to decide when to die; the right of a pregnant woman to decide what should happen within her own body. Or, on the other hand, everybody's right to life, and the corresponding duty of the doctor to preserve it; the right of a living fetus to be born and have a life of its own to live, and the correlative duty of the mother to allow this to happen. The moral issues remain the same, the same moral choices fall to be made. My question in this chapter is What difference does it make to the idea of the moral, if it is expressed in terms of rights? Can there be a real-life alternative theory of morality based on the concept of rights? For at the present time the language of rights is far more widely and confidently used than the simpler language of good and evil.

As a preliminary, I want to get rid of two red herrings. The first is the idea of a 'person'. A person is generally supposed to be a bearer of rights. It is thus often suggested that if we could decide whether an embryo, for example, or a fetus, or a girl in a permanently vegetative state were a person, this would allow us to decide, by rational deduction, whether they had a right to life, or whether we might legitimately cause them to die. It is suggested that there should be certain agreed criteria according to which this decision as to personhood might be fixed, dividing the persons from the non-persons, rather as the criterion of brain-death is (more or less) accepted as the way to determine whether someone is dead or alive. And so various criteria have been suggested. First, it is generally agreed that persons have to be human, that is members of the species *Homo Sapiens*. If distinctions between species are held to be arbitrary or flexible, then of course this criterion might also become flexible: an upright, language-using visitor from Mars or a particularly bright ape might one day have to be admitted as a virtual man, and thus become eligible to be a person. (This has a bearing on the question whether animals can be said to have rights, on which I shall have more to say later.) But there are further criteria: a person, it is often said, must be able to have interests, and to recognise that some things are, some are not in his interest; he must be able to think of himself as one being, with a past and a future; he must be able to recognise himself as a member of a species who can be treated either well or ill, and, especially, justly or unjustly; he must be able to make rational choices; and finally he must have rights which other animals do not have. This last suggested criterion obviously exposes the full circularity of the argument. Deciding whether someone is or is not a person is not like deciding whether he is fair-skinned or dark-skinned, taller than average or shorter than average.

It is to accord him a certain status, as a bearer of rights. There is no way in which one could scientifically classify animals, and discover which were and which were not persons. To talk about personhood is to enter a new kind of discourse.

Everyone who tries to come up with factual or scientific criteria for personhood gets into difficulties over what we are to say about infants or those who, though they once satisfied the criteria, are no longer able to do so, such as those in a coma, or suffering from dementia. But this is not just a little local difficulty. It is fundamental. For it is essentially for society to *decide* who is a bearer of rights. There is no way of looking at the facts about, say, a demented woman, and deducing whether she is a person. In the seventeenth century, John Locke said that 'Person' is a forensic term; and he was right. So deciding who has rights is the very same decision as deciding who is to count as a person. It is a matter for lawyers. We cannot therefore help ourselves to solve the former question by first answering the latter. They are the same. To try to invoke the notion of personhood in discussing the rights of embryos or of the dying, of pregnant women or of fetuses, is a confusing and obfuscating red herring.

The second red herring is perhaps rather less often dragged across the scene. It is the idea of ownership. Defenders of euthanasia may argue that they own their bodies, and have a right, therefore, to dispose of them. Women are prone to say that they own their bodies, and that therefore they have rights over them, and all that is in them. And in some ways this seems quite plausible. We may feel certain that, if we speak of 'my' hand, or 'my' leg, this indicates that the hand or the leg is mine, in the same way as my house or my handbag is mine.

But first we have to notice that 'my' can be used in many different senses, not all of which signify ownership. I do not own my piano teacher or my psychiatrist, though each is intelligibly mine. More relevantly, I do not own my children, once they are born, though a special relationship of a different kind is indicated when I speak of them as 'mine'. But secondly, even of my body, or parts of my body, it is dubious whether I can be said to own them. Suppose I have just given birth, and the placenta has not yet been removed. It is still inside my body. Do I own it; and if at that moment I do, do I continue to own it when it has left my body? There are some American birth-clinics who send the new mother home with the placenta in a bag, on the grounds that it is hers. This may become an increasingly important issue, if scientists can get useful, even highly profitable information from the examination of discarded tissue. There was a notorious case in California (*Moore* v. *Regents of the University of California*, 1990) where the university was sued because it had allegedly made millions of dollars out of developing some self-renewing cells, removed originally from the spleen of a man who had undergone surgery, and who had not thought to claim his discarded spleen as his own. My view is that we should not deploy the concept of ownership in the case of body-parts or tissue, whether still-functioning parts or discarded, even though the notion of a 'gift', or 'donation', may continue to be used in their regard. But in any case this, like the concept of the 'person', is essentially a forensic or legal matter, and cannot be treated as a separate issue from the issue of rights. Rights cannot be deduced on the grounds that my body is mine. If I am deemed to own my body, or parts of it, then I have rights over it. But both questions are, together, up for settlement. This, then, is my second red herring.

Let us turn to the question of rights themselves, and whether they could form the basis of morality. A right is something you claim, and which you can properly prevent other people from infringing. It is an area of freedom for an individual which someone else must allow him to exercise, as a matter of justice. We must consider how the possession of a right is to be established, how a claim to a right is to be upheld, and what precisely is involved in the statement that an entitlement to something, a right, exists. There has been a marked shift in the concept of rights in the last forty years or so, at least in this country. Until about 1960, most people interested in jurisprudence, or the theory of law, whether they were lawyers or philosophers, were broadly what is called legal positivists. Following John Austin and the Utilitarian Jeremy Bentham (both born in the eighteenth century), they held that a right could exist and be claimed only if there existed a law granting that right. If a right had been granted by a law, then other people than the claimant had a duty not to stand in the way of the right's being exercised. Equally, if the law imposed a duty, then someone else had a right against whoever failed to carry out that duty. The simplest example is that of a right of way. However convenient it might be for you to cross my land on the way to work, however much it might be in your interest to do so (avoiding steps, for instance, if you use a wheelchair), however much difference it made to you and how little to me, unless there were a by-law granting a right of way, you could not claim one, nor force me to allow you to cross my land. You might well think I was unreasonable not to allow you to cross it, or unkind or vindictive, and you could accordingly blame me, on moral grounds. I could be accused of being a nasty person, who had no regard to the moral principle that one should help people or love one's neighbour. But there would be no question of rights, or correlative duty on my part. (There is another sense of the word 'duty', in which I might be said to have a moral duty to allow you to cross my land; but I shall return to this later.)

It was Bentham's view, reiterated in everything he wrote, that unless there is a law conferring it, there can be no right. To speak of rights otherwise was 'nonsense on stilts'. This is legal positivism. But of course not all laws are good laws, either because they cannot be enforced, or because the enforcement or the outcome of them is morally objectionable. For instance, though there is a law which gives the police the right to stop and search suspected terrorists, many people hold that it is not right (morally right) that they should be empowered to do so.

Such people do not deny that there exists a law which gives the police this right, but they think it a bad, immoral law, impinging on people's valued freedom to walk about the streets unmolested. If you feel inclined to claim that you have a right not to be stopped and searched, which, as the law stands, you do not have, what you mean, and what in the interests of clarity you should say, is that you ought to have that right; there ought to be a law entitling you to something that you value on moral grounds, namely to be able to walk the streets unmolested. You can campaign to get the present law changed so that you get what ought to be your right. But you cannot claim that it *is* your right. Bentham's motto was 'Obey immediately; criticise ceaselessly.' He thought that the claim to a right where no law conferred it was a piece of damaging rhetoric; and there is, in my opinion, a great deal to be said for his view.

A good example, capable of clear expression in these Benthamite terms, is that of the Education Act of 1972, to which I have already referred, which brought the most severely disabled children under the jurisdiction of the then Department of Education and Science, and thus gave them the right to education. It was only by the new legislation that these children were accorded that right. Positivists would say that, until 1972, the children had no right to education (largely, of course, because hardly anyone thought that education was possible for them, a somewhat narrow view of education being assumed, that it had to do only with numeracy and literacy). But there were enlightened people about, who realised that severely disabled children ought to have a right to education, and that therefore there ought to be a law entitling them to it, and accordingly the law was changed. Here is a case, then, which can well be presented in positivist terms, a sharp distinction being drawn between the law as it is and the law as it ought to be (and in this case has become). To speak thus is to give morality priority over rights. It must be in terms of pre-existing morality that laws (and therefore rights) can be criticised. Therefore morality cannot be derived from rights, as a matter of logic.

It is sometimes held that rights may be engendered not by any specific law, but by a person's absolute *need*, the satisfaction of which constitutes not merely something he desires, but something to which he is entitled. It is certainly true that there is a connection between a perceived need and a right. And it was for this reason that the report following the enquiry into the education of disabled children introduced the concept of special educational needs, emphasising the rights these children now had to education. But in fact the concept of a need is slippery. Even at the very beginning of the Welfare State, with the Beveridge Report, William Beveridge recognised that the welfare ideal, for the state to meet the basic needs of everyone equally, would change over time, and would eventually escalate so that it could hardly be afforded (though I doubt whether he foresaw the scale of the erosion of welfarism, or that it would come so soon). What counts as an absolute need is relative to what is seen to be an intolerable or impossible way to live (i.e. if the need is not met). And to make a judgement as to what is intolerable is, in my view, to make a moral judgement. So even if needs do generate rights, still the idea of the morally good and the morally bad precede these rights. (For a detailed discussion of the concept of needs, see David Wiggins, *Needs, Values, Truth*, Blackwell, 1987, chapter 1.)

However that may be, for largely extraneous reasons such as the increasingly perceived inadequacy of the Benthamite 'greatest happiness' principle (a moral theory which seemed to offer moral justification for sacrificing individuals to a kind of collective good, and whose insistence on criticising laws by the criterion of maximising overall good even at the expense of the good of individuals was properly seen as inadequate) legal positivism as a whole began to be frowned on. It seemed to set up a false and unrealistic barrier between law and morality. It appeared to encourage people (in Nazi Germany, for example) to rely on the concept of *Gesetz als Gesetz* (the Law as Law) and therefore to have supported German lawyers in their failure to protest at the enormities they were required to perpetrate in the name of the law. It has therefore become more common to incorporate the idea of certain inalienable human rights into the idea of law itself, giving the law an intrinsically moral content. A legal system cannot be justified, it is argued, unless it is firmly based on an already existing, and logically prior, concept of human rights, a concept from which not only law but morality itself stems. If a law was changed, it was changed in the light of these inalienable human rights which preceded it. Thus old laws gave masters legal rights over their slaves. The abolition of slavery recognised pre-existing rights; it did not create them. Similarly, the 1972 legislation entitling all children to education recognised a right already belonging to all human beings, the right to be educated. I think that this new anti-positivist concept of law is fraught with confusion; but it is necessary to try to understand it, if we are to understand the present insistence on rights as the only aspect of morality that has a 'cutting edge'.

In reality things are not as simple as I (or Bentham) have made out. Laws, being in their nature general, are nearly always, in real life, subject to interpretation. I borrow the following example from H.L.A. Hart (see, for example, 'Positivism and the Separation of Law and Morals', *Harvard Law Review*, 1958). Suppose there is a by-law which forbids taking vehicles into a public park. There are some things we would all agree counted as vehicles, such as cars or tanks. More dubious might be an ice-cream van. What about a helicopter, or a skate-board? In working out whether the by-law has been breached, the adjudicator (let us say the magistrate) has to make a decision. It is not a matter of simple deduction of the form 'Vehicles are forbidden; skate-boards are vehicles; therefore skate-boards are forbidden.' For the purposes of the Act, the magistrate may deem that skate-boards are, or are not, vehicles. Let us suppose that he decides that they are not vehicles and are to be allowed in the park. On what grounds does he base his decision? We have very little temptation to say that he has recognised a certain inalienable human right, existing since the beginning of time, to bring skate-boards into the park. On the contrary, the magistrate has plainly *created* a right. Hereafter if you go into the park with your skate-board and are challenged by the park-keeper, you can claim that you are entitled to do so. Usually, and in this case, when such an interpretative decision is taken it is based on a consideration of what the law was *for*. In this case, the purpose of the law was to protect people who wanted to enjoy the park free from disturbance or danger. It was probably with this in mind that the magistrate decided that skate-boards were not vehicles. Although they carried people on wheels, which is the proper function of vehicles, they were not noisy, did not create polluting fumes, and did not often knock people over.

Now though this is a case where comfort, convenience and safety are involved, rather than any strictly moral issues, I think it may cast some light on the relation between morality and the law. In the case of the 1972 Education Act, the law was extended so that all children became entitled to education, not merely those not severely disabled. The change would not have come about unless there had been people who believed on moral grounds and with passionate conviction that it was wrong to deprive any child of that from which he could benefit, as we now knew that he could. Looking on the law which compelled people to send their children to school, it was clear that the purpose of the law was to ensure that no child who could benefit from education should be deprived of it. What had changed, according to the campaigners, was the concept of education itself, and consequently the notion of who could benefit. Their moral conviction was based on the new knowledge that education could make an enormous difference to the quality of life of even the most severely disabled, therefore, morally speaking, we must provide what education could be afforded. It is my contention that we should not think of such moral convictions as these, which lie behind the law, and without which the law would not be changed, in terms of rights. We can express them simply in terms of humanity, the way we ought to treat human children, sentiments which motivated the original laws compelling parents to have their children educated. This is analogous to the decision of the magistrate, described above, who decided to allow skate-boards into the park, by reference to the purpose of the original by-law. Rights did not come into the matter until he created your right to bring your skateboard in. Before that, all you could have argued would have been that you *ought* to have been allowed to bring them in, because they were safe and non-disturbing, which was in accordance with the spirit of the original by-law.

Some might argue that the old education law, which excluded certain children from education, was changed on the ground that it was unjust, or unfair; and that this entails a pre-existing right for all children to be treated equally.

For it is only the infringement of rights that constitutes injustice. Therefore the rights must have existed before the law was changed. However, it is far from clear what is meant by invoking equality in this context (though I have been inclined to invoke it myself – see Introduction). The reason why some children were excluded from education before 1972 was that they were held to be, as a matter of fact, ineducable (and this because of a limited view of the content of education prevailing theretofore). In this sense these children could not be treated as the equals of their contemporaries. They might properly have been classed metaphorically, as I have noticed, as 'vegetables', a description certainly not appropriate for all children equally. It would be no more a requirement of equality to try to educate them than it would be to try to teach me, unlike some of my contemporaries, to become an opera singer or a ballet dancer.

However, the claim that all children have a right to be treated equally may be the expression of a more general claim, namely that all humans, in a civil society, have a right to be treated equally under the system of laws in that society. Such a notion of equality is the very foundation of law and justice. But what precisely this entitles them to will depend on the content of the law. Before 1972, a parent could not sue a local authority for not providing education for her severely handicapped child, since that was not part of their legal duties. After that she could sue. Before 1972 the discrimination of which she might want to complain was not unfair discrimination; it was legal, the criteria laid down by the law. Only after 1972 did it become possible to argue that, if a severely handicapped child, or indeed any child, had not been educated, he had suffered injustice. Before 1972, what a parent needed was a stance from which she could criticise the law. It is my contention that this stance is a moral stance. The parent who complains is adopting a moral, not a legal standpoint.

However, it is sometimes argued that, apart from the positive laws which currently create rights, there is a higher law from which higher rights may be derived (and this might include the higher right of all children to equal treatment, educationally, not granted them in the pre-1972 legislation). Thus Sophocles represents Antigone, determined to show respect for her brother by throwing earth on his body, claiming a right to do this, though it was forbidden by existing law. In her great speech to Kreon, the Theban tyrant, she invokes a higher, divine law, under which she has the right to honour her brother, and indeed is obliged by the law to do so. Similarly, appeals to natural law or natural justice may give rise to the concept of natural rights, or universal human rights, one of which, it might be claimed, was the right to education. Injustice, where a child is debarred from education, would be an offence against such higher law. But one may properly ask what natural law is. If it is that fundamental principle of justice which is the underlying basis of all positive law, then it seems to me plain that it should be referred to as a moral principle, derived from the needs and the aspirations of human nature. It is indeed the basis from which one may criticise all positive laws. To adopt this way of speaking of natural law, as a fundamental *moral* principle, is to distinguish the moral from the legal, and to derive the legal from the moral. If someone claims a natural right, according to this way of speaking, he would be claiming a moral right, and invoking a moral law or principle as the source of this right. There is no doubt in my mind that such a manner of claiming rights would greatly lessen the confusion we now find ourselves in, and would firmly establish the priority of the moral over the legal.

However, if the rights are moral, not legal, and if the law conferring them is a moral law, then the necessity for using the language of rights seems to disappear. Why should we not prefer simply to talk about ways in which it would be right or wrong, good or bad, to treat our fellow humans? This would be to adopt the language of morality itself, with no quasi-legal implications.

The drawback of using the language of rights in so very general and abstract a context is, as I shall hope to show, that more and more may be claimed as a natural or fundamental human right, even where such claims are dubious and may be disputed. We are accustomed to fundamental disagreements about morality. So if I claim that such and such is a moral principle, you may be ready to say that I have got the principle wrong, or that it is a matter of mere convention, not of morality. But if, on the other hand, I claim that something is a right, then there is an air of certainty, borrowed from the positivist sense of 'right', an implication that the right could be proved (as in the case of a right of way). This is to say that, even if there is a case to be made for talking about a 'human', 'natural' or 'moral' right, for example to education, or to justice itself, the idea of such rights should be extended only with caution, since the word 'right' has such vast rhetorical power: and the power is largely borrowed from its narrower use, within the confines of an existing system of law. For, as I have said, to claim that your rights have been violated is to claim that you have been unjustly treated. And in civilised, as opposed to primitive societies, a claim to unjust treatment constitutes an imperative. Justice *must* be done.

Because we are increasingly aware of the immoral and barbarous ways in which people may be treated under various political regimes, of the appalling cruelty inherent in ideological dogmatism, and of the peculiar horrors which follow political coups or civil wars, we are more and more inclined to refer, in such cases, to the violation of human rights. And, very properly, this goes along with the attempt to establish new supranational systems of law, which will incorporate not only the fundamental imperative that people should be treated fairly, but also that they shall not be subjected to things which manifestly damage them, when they are innocent of any harm: they must not be imprisoned without trial, massacred or driven from their homes; they must not be subjected to gross cruelty, such as torture or deliberate starvation. The value of such a system of law is held to be that where it has been infringed, in theory at least, the perpetrators of the infringement can be brought to a court; and the people damaged by the infringement can claim that it is their rights that have been infringed just insofar as these rights are specified in the system of law. The birth of the United Nations, after the Second World War, was marked by the issue of the Universal Declaration of Human Rights which specified most of the rights which were to be protected. This declaration was not recognised as part of International Law. However, increasingly human rights issues are considered to be part either of international treaties and conventions, or of the general principles of law recognised by civilised countries, and there are various regional conventions which have established machinery through which complaints of violation may be heard. I would argue that, at this level of generality, it is impossible to distinguish between law and morality; legal positivism, with its Benthamite insistence on distinguishing the two, has no place. For these general principles consist not only in the basic principle of justice, that everyone should be equal before the law, but also the principles forbidding outrageous and inhumane treatment of numerous different kinds, some of which I have just listed. There is therefore an inextricable weaving together of legal and moral terminology in the discussion of human rights issues. And though it may well be that the rhetoric of rights and their violation has a useful function at this kind of level, there are nevertheless certain cautions that should be observed. The risk of devaluing the currency of rights-claims is, as I have suggested, something to be avoided.

For example, even where someone has an undoubted legal right to some treatment, say to have certain basic health needs met by a health service in a Welfare State, it may not always be possible to ensure that the treatment is at hand, or the needs satisfied. To take an extreme, but by no means impossible case: suppose there has been some disaster, such as an earthquake, and a large number of people are buried in the ruins. Each of these people is entitled, in the Welfare State, to medical treatment according to their needs, and some of them will need blood transfusions. If there is a shortage of blood of a particular blood group, then a person who is uncovered from the ruins may find that all the blood of her group has been used up on people who were rescued earlier. She is entitled to a blood transfusion, but cannot have one. The proper and normal reaction (as David Wiggins pointed out, op. cit., p. 29) to someone's rights being infringed is one of indignation; but in this case there is no cause for indignation, only for sorrow or pity. Everyone did their best, but it ended in tragedy. There is simply no point in reiterating that the victim had a right to have a transfusion.

There is another obvious caution. Whenever a right is claimed one is entitled, as I have argued, to raise the question Who or what conferred it? If the answer is that no one conferred it, nor did it arise out of any contract or agreement, it is a right simply intrinsic to the condition of being human, then one must try to be certain that something is not claimed as an absolute right, for all humans and for all time, which is in fact to be thought of as a right only at a specific time, in specific circumstances and for some people, not others. For example in 1990 the United Kingdom signed the UNICEF charter of children's rights, and later ratified its signature. The purpose of this charter was to entitle all children equally and everywhere to have their basic needs met, needs incurred first because they were human and secondly because they were children. Article 6 of the convention which constitutes the charter lays down that 'every child has the inherent right to life'. But does this mean that absolutely every baby that is born, however slim its chances of survival, however poor will be the quality of its future life, while it lasts, has the right to have everything done that can be done to keep it alive? Is it always an infringement of rights if a paediatrician, or indeed a parent, switches the life-support machine off? What if not all badly damaged neonates *can* be saved, because of the shortage of cots in the intensive care unit? Consideration of such cases as these makes it seem that the right to life is a pretty vague sort of right, for it must often be overridden by other considerations, moral, administrative or financial. Again, if we look at the words of the convention, we find that children must be brought up in their families; that they must not work; that they must be educated, and educated in a particular way, 'to understand human rights'; that they must have the opportunity to play and to exercise their imaginations in the arts and in free speech. All this is doubtless excellent; but we ought to be clear that the convention is putting forward an ideal of childhood such as is generally enjoyed by children in liberal Western societies, which are prosperous, and where childhood can therefore be prolonged. Even if we embrace this ideal, and attempt to realise it for as many children as possible, it is straining the concept of a right to suggest that for every child whose childhood is not like this there is a positive breach of duty on someone's part, or on the part of that society in which the child grows up. I do not deny that the ideal of childhood set out in the convention is good. In particular, I believe that there is much to be said for a long, irresponsible protected childhood. But in thinking of this we have moved a long way from basic needs or intrinsic rights. Such a childhood has always been a function of affluence, or relative affluence. It does not seem to make much sense to say that every child has a right to be born into an affluent family. The trouble is that if the language of rights is used to describe such ideals, morally excellent though they may be, that language is devalued.

A right should remain something which, even if it is not ensured by enforceable law (as a right of way, or a right to legally held property is), yet is such that it *might* be ensured, if an agreed law or convention could be found. Such are human rights, as laid down in the United Nations charter. For it is by now fairly well agreed what it means to say of a particular state that it has a 'bad human rights record'. What is less clear is to what extent infringement of human rights may be the trigger for action, whether military or legal. In any case the charter of children's rights comes nowhere near this level of agreement; and it is for this reason that I believe such language should be abandoned, lest the coinage become debased.

The case for avoiding the language of rights is even stronger in the matter of so-called animal rights. Just as there exists legislation criminalising cruelty and abuse of children so, for more than a century, there has been legislation protective of animals. The Cruelty to Animals Act 1856 was for more than a century the Act under which people could be charged with mistreating animals, in an increasingly varying context. Originally it was designed to outlaw manifestly cruel treatment of animals in circuses, in side-shows, on farms, and especially in the streets. It was the outcome of much campaigning, largely against cruel cabbies, who starved and flogged their aged horses, under the public eye. Anna Sewell's *Black Beauty* was an effective weapon in the armoury of the anti-cruelty lobby, and horses were accorded a special place in the Act (which was one of the factors which made the Act so inappropriate as a measure to deal with the treatment of laboratory animals, in the second half of the twentieth century). The Cruelty to Animals Act remains on the statute book, but is now joined by the legislation, dating from 1985, regulating the use of animals in scientific experimentation, which lays down that scientists using animals must be registered, their laboratories and holding-houses subject to inspection; that the use of animals must be shown to be essential; that animals must not be used repeatedly for experiment; that animals must be supplied from recognised supply sources; and that if an animal is in severe pain that is likely to continue, the research project must be halted even if unfinished, and the animal destroyed. Now both of these Acts of Parliament could, I suppose, be interpreted as conferring on the animals some negative rights, rights not to be, in some specified ways, maltreated. In the same way, one could interpret legislation against burglary or against allowing pollution to flow into a river as conferring rights on people in general not to be burgled, or not to be at risk from polluted water, or from piles of dead fish. But though, especially in the last case, people might bring an action against the polluter, this would be on account of damage suffered rather than of rights infringed. In the same way both the old and the new legislation regarding the treatment of animals is most readily understood as forbidding certain practices regarded as morally intolerable, and criminalising these practices, not as upholding any rights. Indeed the basic assumptions of both laws are the same, namely that it is perfectly acceptable that animals should be used by humans for various purposes, for instance to produce milk, to draw vehicles, to test drugs, to help to uncover some of the mysteries of reproduction and embryonic growth. The law questions none of these things. All it prohibits is the occasioning, in the course of these transactions, of unnecessary suffering. The infringement of a right is, as I have emphasised, essentially an act of *injustice*. The infringement of the laws which protect animals is an act of *cruelty*, or, in the case, for example, of infringement of licensing regulations, is an act thought liable to make cruelty more probable, and easier to get away with.

Those who proclaim that animals have rights start by saying that the present laws protecting animals are inadequate; and in this they doubtless have a point. For there are still many ways in which animals can be cruelly treated, in transport, for example, or in battery-farming, which fall outside the legislation. But if they mean more than this, namely that the basic presupposition of the laws is mistaken, then they must show that animals are entitled not to be used for human purposes, just as one human may not be used for the purposes of another, without infringing the basic entitlement to equality which is the moral principle lying behind all law.

I am not certain how far the defenders of animal rights would wish to go along these lines. Most of them would argue that animals should not be bred for the table, cooked and eaten. But may they be milked for human purposes? Some say yes, some no. May they be ridden? If ridden, then raced? May they be hunted? To this the answer is no, not by humans; but presumably their rights are not infringed if they are hunted by animals other than humans. And here the real difficulties start. If all animals had a right to freedom to live their lives without molestation, then someone would have to protect them from one another. But this is absurd. Even if it were agreed that humans should not own or breed or eat or milk animals, so that all cattle would revert to the wild, nothing could be done to alter the fact that animals are feral. If freed from the bonds imposed on them by men, they would not live in a civil society, within which rights and duties would arise. They would live in the state of nature. The rights claimed for them are rights only against humans, it is only humans who could have duties towards them. Yet it is impossible to believe (for me at least) that humans could admit animals into civil society on equal terms. For a civil society is essentially one in which rights and duties are *recognised*. Caligula may have made his horse consul, but it is not to be imagined that he expected much in the way of administrative performance from him. I may give my cat the freedom to come and go as he pleases, by putting in a cat-flap; but I do not extend his freedom much beyond this. I am just as ruthless as before in throwing out the half-dead mice and birds that he may choose to bring into the kitchen, and I never even wonder whether I am infringing a right. We live on my terms. He is my property. If I get too poor to keep him, I give him away, or put him to death.

There is no possible way to suppose that we may treat humans like this. However, in expressing such sentiments, I will be accused by some of demonstrating 'speciesism' (see for example Peter Singer, *Practical Ethics*, Cambridge, 1979), an irrational prejudice in favour of the human over other species. I would freely acknowledge that, in my view, humans have moral priority over other animals. I would think it morally outrageous if someone preferred, faced with a choice, to save their dog rather than their even severely handicapped baby. It is humans and they alone who can form a civil society within which the concepts of rights and duties arise. That some people cannot, and may never be able to, recognise these rights and duties (like perhaps the severely handicapped baby) does not entail that this baby is not part of human society. What I would deny is that this is an irrational prejudice, like racism or sexism. It is, instead, the foundation of all morality.

To speak of the rights of animals, then, is necessarily inappropriate, simply because 'animal' here means 'animal other than human'. And to use the language of rights in this context is dangerously to debase the currency of rights. It is morally wrong to treat animals with cruelty, and this is the force of the relevant criminal law. Moreover it is precisely because humans are fundamentally different from other animals that they have an obligation not to treat them with cruelty. Other animals can have no such obligation one to another, across species, for they could not conceive of the world of nature as a whole, nor have any global view of what would be bad or degrading behaviour within that world. Indeed, it is not only the avoidance of cruelty to animals that is a human obligation. There is a wider concept, which may be encapsulated in the word 'respect', though the word is not wholly adequate. Because humans have an idea of themselves as part of, though in a sense aliens in, the world of nature, they have an obligation to respect nature, not deliberately or wantonly to destroy it or demean it, perhaps actively to try to conserve it, to admire and love its variety and diversity. The more powerful humans become in manipulating their world for their own ends, the greater the danger to other species both of other animals and of plants. Equally, the more we know about nature, the more marvellous and also the more precarious we see it to be. It is from these twin phenomena that we increasingly feel our human duty of respect, a duty which self-evidently falls on (as it is recognised by) none but humans. It is difficult to find words accurately to describe this proper relation between man and the rest of nature. The metaphor of stewardship, deriving from a long Judaeo-Christian tradition, perhaps brings out the flavour best. As often happens, a moral concept is best expressed in religious language, and is difficult to translate out of that language without loss. Certainly for anyone whose first glimpses of morality came through religion, the metaphor is self-explanatory. But that we are in the position of stewards, that we have duties to the rest of nature, in no way entails that nature has rights against us. And this leads to the central point that I would make about rights and duties.

There is obviously a sense in which rights and duties are linked. If someone claims a legal right, then this entails that someone has a duty to see that the right is respected. Such is the basis of all contracts, and all legislation enacted specifically to protect particular rights. It is the relative precision of this relationship that I want to defend. Though I have conceded that there may be a certain usefulness, or effectiveness, in talking about fundamental human rights, rights which belong necessarily to all human beings, even where no contract has been made, and no detailed legislation put in place, yet I have argued that it is mere rhetoric to try to extend these rights beyond a few that would be agreed to be basic. This is true whether the charter of human rights is supposed to be observed globally, within Europe, or within the United Kingdom. And even to specify such rights as these is really to specify kinds of behaviour towards human beings, or kinds of restrictions of freedom which are generally agreed to be morally outrageous. It is because of my fear of a debasement of the powerful currency of rights that I deplore widening the scope of the concept. In particular I deplore the thoughtless issuing, towards the end of the twentieth century, of so-called charters, the parents' charter, the rail-users' charter, the patients' charter. These charters have never been agreed; they seem to confer rights, but they have not the force of law. They dangerously raise the expectations of parents, rail-users or patients that they may claim what they are promised as their due. Of course it is good to set out what the various services hope to provide. But this is very different from issuing a charter of rights.

In despair the National Health Service has started to argue that the patients' charter entails duties as well as rights for patients. But this is based on a total confusion. If rights and duties are correlative, as I have argued, it is in the sense that the right of a patient to treatment entails the duty of the health service to provide it. It is not the case that no one can have a right who does not *himself* have some duty, though this may be so in the case of contracts (as where I have a right to have my roof properly mended, so long as I fulfil my duty to pay the agreed charge). Infants can have rights, though they have no duties. But the poor health service is now saying that the patients' charter entails the duty on patients not to call out their doctors on frivolous grounds, or not to put their feet on the chairs in the waiting area. This was never part of the charter, which was unconditional. And what are the conditions supposed to be implied in the rail-users' charter? That they should be clean, sober and orderly, and not put their feet on the seat opposite in the carriage? This was never stated.

This is simply an example of the way that the relation between rights and duties may be misunderstood. It is also an example of an increasing tendency to believe that everything desirable may be claimed as a right. It is the very same tendency that was exemplified in the International Declaration of Children's Rights. It is one thing, and often a good thing, to publish an ideal to be aspired to; quite another to publish a charter of rights.

The essential distinction between moral ideals, and rights with correlative duties, convinces me that there cannot be a morality *founded* on the concept of rights. The infringement of a right is always a case of injustice. But avoiding injustice is only one way of achieving moral good, or avoiding evil. Judith Jarvis Thomson, in an article on abortion ('A defense of abortion' reprinted in her *Rights, Restitution and Risk*, ed. William Parent, Princeton University Press, 1986) makes the point in this way. A box of chocolates has been given to the older of two brothers. 'There he sits, stolidly eating his way through the box, his small brother watching enviously. Here we are likely to say, "You ought not to be so mean. You ought to give your brother some of those chocolates." My own view is that it just does not follow from the truth of this that the brother has any right to any of the chocolates. If the boy refuses to give his brother any, he is greedy, stingy, callous – but not unjust. [Some people] will say that it does follow that the brother has a right to some of the chocolates, and thus that the boy does act unjustly if he refuses to give his brother any. But the effect of saying this is to obscure what we should keep distinct, namely the difference between this case and the boy's refusal in a case in which the box was given to both boys jointly, and in which the small brother thus has what is from any point of view clear title to half.' I agree with her entirely. To say, on moral grounds, that someone *ought* to behave in a particular way may have nothing whatever to do with the justice of his doing so. To avoid cruelty is not, or not necessarily, the same as to avoid injustice; and greed, callousness, lack of human sympathy are all different moral vices.

In Victorian and Edwardian days, perhaps even in the Georgian days of my own childhood (though I suspect less confidently), the word 'duty' was used to denote what you ought to do, how you ought to behave, in a perfectly general sense. I suppose the duties were thought to be imposed on you by laws, the Ten Commandments, perhaps, or the more positive and more general laws of the New Testament. Some of the duties were implicit in a particular position you occupied (as an officer and a gentleman, for example, or as the lady of the manor). The Oxford philosopher F.H. Bradley entitled one of the chapters of his book on ethics (*Ethics*, Oxford, 1899) 'My Station and its Duties'. The point about such duties is that in no sense did they imply any correlative rights. If I take soup to the poor in the village, or run the Sunday school, or send peaches from my conservatory to the tenants who are sick, they have no right to these good things, even if, because of my benevolence, they may come to expect, even to rely on them. What they may feel, if they are given to such feelings, is gratitude (but they may equally feel humiliation or envy). They will not feel that they have got only what it is their right to have. I, on my side, may act so because I conceive it to be my duty to look after the poor; but my motives may be, as well, compassion, pity or generosity. In the old use of the word 'duty', no such motives were excluded; indeed they were motives by which you *ought* to be activated. A dutiful person was a person who did what was right, and wanted to be good.

This general use of the word 'duty' is connected, necessarily, with a general use of 'obligation'. Some obligations arise out of specific tasks or roles we have, such as that of parent, or teacher, or park-warden. Here the obligations may be specified in a job description, but may more extensively be simply understood to belong to the role in question. In becoming a parent, you are generally agreed to incur obligations. Again, some obligations are deliberately taken on by promising. If you promise, you state an intention to do something, in a particularly binding way. You not only create an expectation in the person to whom you make the promise, that you will do what you say you will, but, in binding yourself to do it, you give him the *right* to expect that you will. This is the strictest sense of the word 'obligation', and it matches the strict sense of the word 'duty'. But apart from these cases, there are many more when we may speak of *feeling* obliged. And here we are appealing to a moral sense which may have nothing to do either with the particular obligations arising out of a job or a status, or with a specific undertaking by which you deliberately bound yourself to do what you said you would do. This sense of obligation may arise because you feel that you must act in a particular way. You *have* to. Such was the obligation, in the first story (see Chapter One), that the doctor felt to relieve the suffering of his dying patient. Such may be the obligation I feel to help someone who has incurred my gratitude by helping me when I needed it.

Such ideas, whether of duty or of obligation, have as their background a settled and stable sense of what is right, and a willingness to submit to a set of principles from which duties and obligations may be derived. It is the virtual disappearance of such a background, and an increasing, but seldom argued, belief that everyone must make his own rules, that has brought the words into varying degrees of disuse. The now out-moded concept of *general* duty and the *feeling* of obligation both belong centrally to the sphere of private morality. We tend to be chary of addressing the question of other people's 'private' moral codes, and to be much more at ease in the public domain, and this is increasingly true. When a right is denied someone, or a freedom he should have is infringed, then justice can be demanded. Justice is easy to demand because it is an essentially public concept. Aristotle discovered, when in the *Nicomachaean Ethics* he attempted to go through and analyse human virtues one by one, that justice sits uneasily among the other virtues. It may be the property of institutions as well as of individuals. It is essentially a civil, not a personal virtue. Justice is an aspect of public morality, indeed is its very foundation, and in speaking of justice Aristotle, and we, move from the private to the public mode.

However central to public morality the ideal of justice may be, there are other aspects of morality, concerned necessarily with individuals, their motives, characters and consciences. A civil society, however scrupulous with regard to the rights of individuals, and the duties of others not to infringe individual rights or inhibit freedoms, cannot be founded on such scruples alone. For to defend a right is to demand something for oneself, or the group to which one belongs. On the other hand private or personal morality is based, not on such self-interested demands, but on the possibility of self-denial or altruism, the thought that others are as important as, or more important than, oneself. In the nursery, our nanny used to look at us threateningly, if we were being greedy or showing off or annoying other people, and say 'T.O.O.' This meant 'Think of Others.' It was not a bad basis for moral education. The moral virtues are objects of admiration, and aspiration, for those who want to be good rather than bad. And this wish, as I have suggested, is essential to morality. If the boy shares the chocolates equally with his brother when they have been given to both, we regard this as only fair; we do not specially admire it. If he fails to share, in those circumstances, then we feel, on his brother's behalf, indignation and resentment. If he shares when the chocolates have been given to him alone, we admire him. He is Thinking of Others. He is displaying sympathy, kindness and generosity. It is my contention that a civil society could not function if it subsisted only on indignation where rights had been infringed, without the occasion for admiration as well for those who, like the Good Samaritan, go out of their way to display altruism. If justice were the only, or even the most fundamental, value, such ideas as compassion, or hatred of cruelty, or shame at dishonesty might wither away. It would be an impoverished, because an essentially public, morality that was founded on the concept of rights. Even to feel indignation when the rights of others are infringed, rather than our own, though this is a moral indignation, is not the only moral sentiment we are capable of feeling, nor the most fundamental. For it may be divorced from any feeling that we want to be good, *ourselves*. It is easy to inveigh against countries with 'a bad human rights record', which do not impinge on us. We can adopt such a stance while neglecting more domestic wrongs. It is my contention that we neglect private morality at our peril. Having thus contrasted the public and the private, however, it is time now, in the next chapter, to say a bit more about the nature of private morality itself.

Where Ethics Comes From

Anyone who has followed this book so far will realise that I am hostile to the idea of a rights-based morality. In my original stories, concerned with death and life, what was at issue was the most deeply felt sentiments that human beings can experience (and this was why I started with death and birth). Ethical issues were indisputably at the heart of the arguments about these cases, and were as much to be felt in the guts as to be disputed in the law courts, which is where rights must be properly upheld. What is public is what is needed to establish law and justice in civil society, to which belong the concepts of the rights of individuals and the duties of others to respect and uphold those rights. Within public morality, all humans are equal, whatever their individual characteristics; for to maintain this is the crucial function of the institutions within which rights may be claimed and recognised. What is private, on the other hand, is the inner sense of and interest in what it is to do right rather than wrong, an interest in morality itself, what I have referred to as the wish to be good. Looking around us, we can see that some people have this wish strongly, others have it weakly, or not at all. We may feel tempted to borrow Jane Austen's phrase and say that there are those who 'feel as they ought'; they have, that is to say, a moral sense; and it is to this moral sense that I have accorded priority.

Now in giving priority to the private over the public, I do not claim that every civil society has historically been built on such a private, individual interest in the morally good. Such a suggestion might well be false; and in any case we could have no evidence either of its truth or its falsity. But I maintain that public morality, the insistence on justice and equality, the search for a publicly accept-able solution to dilemmas on which opinions may differ, and yet where legislation is required, is dependent for its working on the conviction of at least some individuals that it is worth being virtuous rather than vicious, honest rather than dishonest, good rather than bad: that one must try, individually as well as collectively, to act for the best. We have now to ask where such convictions come from.

A sceptical reader may say that, though some people certainly appear to believe that they should follow the path of the good rather than the bad, how can we be sure that they are not simply deluded? I seem to be making an enormous assumption, if I am claiming that there is such a thing as the morally good as distinct from the morally bad, towards which it makes sense for individuals to aspire. Anyone hoping for a guide to ethics will seize on this assumption, and will demand that it be shown to have proper grounds. In the past, they will say, it might have been all right to leave the assumption unexamined, for most people might have agreed that religion, in the form of the commands of God, defined the sphere of the moral, and Holy Writ (the Bible or some other) proved that there was such a thing as good and evil, introducing people to the notion of such distinctions, to which they then clung. But the radical secularisation of societies, conspicuously our own, makes it essential, if we are to continue to talk about the morally good and its opposite, that we should justify such language, and show that it is not simply a left-over, a kind of scent hanging in the air after the demise of generally accepted religion. The philosopher John McKie, for example, in his book, *Ethics – Inventing Right and Wrong* (Harmondsworth, 1977) argued that this is what ethics consists in, a device which was found serviceable, in the days when religion could reinforce its precepts, and has now been reinvented with a vocabulary which borrows its authority from its old, abandoned, source. No one, he argued, could claim that ethical statements are *true* without being guilty of an actual mistake. He called his theory, accordingly, an 'error theory' of ethics. I shall not concern myself with the details of McKie's argument, but shall try to address the question of what the moral is, what we are talking about when we assert that some things are morally good, some bad, in terms that will be intelligible to everyone, not just to those who profess a religious faith, nor indeed to those who do not. And so in this chapter I shall try to answer two, related, questions: What is morality? and Where does it come from?

With the secularisation of society, these questions are

urgent and central, an answer to them properly demanded by one following a guide to ethics. Yet, as I said in my introductory remarks, they are a sort of question seldom asked by philosophers, whose province they might be thought to be, in the first sixty years or so of this century. G.E. Moore had held that there were *no* grounds for moral judgements or for moral decisions. One simply had to see what was good and one would go for it. The good was self-evidently to be pursued. Fundamental moral concepts could be neither derived nor defined. 'Good is good and that is the end of the matter' (*Principia Ethica*, Cambridge, 1903, p. 6). To try to derive or define good was a fallacy, and especially fallacious was the attempt to define it in terms of the nature of things in the world. This was to commit the sin of Naturalism. One might be forgiven for thinking that Moore's doctrine would make sense only to those who held that moral qualities were supernatural, emanating from God, or somehow from beyond or outside the natural world. For unless one held that faith, what other grounds for the moral could there possibly be except the nature of things, and especially the nature of human beings who alone have a use for the concepts of morality? Moore did not hold this; in his view goodness was a *non*-natural, not a *super*-natural property; and for someone seeking to find a secular ground for distinguishing good from evil, right from wrong, it is exceedingly difficult, I would say impossible, to make sense of this central aspect of his theory. Yet his influence, along with the influence of logical positivism, led to a refusal for many years to address the problems to be addressed in this chapter. The aftermath of logical positivism, as I have already suggested, meant that there was nothing to be said about good and evil, right and wrong themselves, or about what was designated by these terms. One could raise questions only about the sense or otherwise of the language in which we spoke of them. Ethics was just a way of talking, of a peculiar kind. We could investigate the peculiar nature of this language, if we liked. But what ethicists, or moralists, were talking *about* in their special language dropped out of the picture.

However, these theories, vigorous enough for a time, have lost their power to impress. They began to look simply too boring, both to professional philosophers and to their pupils. The actual moral problems in the world became too insistent, and demanded philosophical as well as practical thought. And so we are now entitled to address our question head-on: What is moral discourse about?

First, it is plain that morality has to do with the behaviour of human beings. However horrible or tragic, natural phenomena such as storms or earthquakes are not morally bad or evil; nor is the behaviour of animals other than humans, even if tiresome, obstinate or downright destructive, though, anthropomorphically, we may sometimes speak as though it were.

So we may start by asking whether there is something *about* human beings which makes them, and them alone, the subject-matter of moral discourse. It was Aristotle who most strongly and systematically emphasised that the difference between men and the other living components of the natural world was their possession of rationality. Living things all had souls, or lives. Plants had vegetative life alone; other animals (the brute creation, as it used to be called) had this life and sensitive and perceiving life as well; men alone had a third kind of life, superimposed upon and absorbing the other two, the life of rationality. In an adult, reason took two forms, one superior (more god-like) than the other. Man's god-like or pure reason was concerned with the knowledge and contemplation of features of the world which could not be otherwise. People devoted to the cultivation of pure reason were mathematicians, scientists and philosophers. They could not be expected to give much attention to practical matters. Aristotle observes that Thales, the great scientist-philosopher, was always falling into wells. But, apart from this rarefied form of intellectual life, there was, for everybody, the life of practical reason, concerned with things which were subject to change, ordinary material matters of everyday life, of public policies, or the waging of wars. Practical reason was thus concerned with goal-directed activity. Whether a man chose to pursue good or bad goals was ultimately a matter of his character; but for this character he was partly responsible. For it was possible to develop a good character, as a young man, by practising good acts. In performing good acts, perhaps at first because you were told to do so, or made to feel shame for not doing so, or saw other people whom you admired doing so, you gradually came to see, as it were, the point of them. High standards of behaviour and good goals became, as we might say, internalised. And in the end, the motive of the good man was the good itself. He performed his courageous or fair or honourable actions 'for the sake of the good', or simply because they were good.

At the level of practical reason, human beings had, already given, as part of their ordinary battery of concepts, the idea of good and bad, of virtues and vices. The virtue of a man was his peculiar and appropriate excellence. Whereas the excellence of a horse was its physical powers and perhaps its beauty and skill, so the excellence of a man was his ability to aim deliberately at the practice of the specially human excellences, the virtues of character, or ethical virtues. For Aristotle, then, the idea of ethics could be derived from the nature of the species, human rationality giving rise to the possibility of specifically human virtues, which could recognise themselves for what they were. In every sense, morality, or ethics, was natural; just as an excellent horse performs well, and does not need to be driven or goaded into doing well (wants, for example, to win, when racing), so a good man will not need rewards and punishments to make him act well. He will do so because he wants to, and will take pleasure in it.

The immense difference between Aristotle's answer to the question What is it *about* human beings which makes them the unique subject of ethics? and later answers is of course to be explained by the rise of Christianity. Men as a species are now characterised by their possession not only of reason but of an immortal soul; and they are fitted out with a concept of a God to whom they owe obedience, as well as of a Christ in whose footsteps they ought to follow. The obvious nature of this difference does not prevent its sometimes being overlooked in the history of moral philosophy. Yet Christianity did not mark the end of the view that reason was the unique characteristic which made morality possible for men and for them alone. Rationality, after all, could be seen as the greatest gift that God had endowed men with. So there were still philosophers, even those who held religious views, who sought to make reason the feature of human beings responsible for the existence of the moral. Perhaps the greatest exponent of such a view was Kant.

Aristotle, in all of his philosophy, started from 'the phenomena': what we know about the world we live in, and what we say about it. (If what we know or say seems to lead to contradictions, then is the time for philosophy to sort out what are the most fundamental and unchangeable things we know and say, and discard the rest.) He is sometimes criticised for starting from the ordinary world of perception and language, but where else are we to start? We know and say, and gossip and debate about, the fact that there are good men and bad men; and it was from this point that his Ethics took its starting point. Kant no less than Aristotle began, in his moral philosophy, from where we now are, or at least where he thought we now are.

This meant that for Kant, brought up as a German

Protestant, we must begin to think about ethics from the *fact* that we are surrounded by duties and obligations, things that we know for certain must be done, or must be avoided, according to the dictates of a relentless Protestant conscience, internal to each one of us. His question was How is this certainty, and the positive requirement to act upon it, possible? Where (as we are now asking, in this chapter) did such certainty come from? His answer, in the *Critique of Practical Reason* and in the *Grundlegung* (*The Fundamental Principles of the Metaphysic of Ethics*), was that it came from human reason itself. To act under necessity, as one does when obeying the dictates of conscience, is to act according to a law. The whole of nature is subject to laws, and every change in nature, as we perceive it, is, according to Kant, subject to some causal law. Rational creatures, however, are subject not merely to the physical laws which govern the behaviour of all material objects, but, uniquely, to moral laws as well, which it is the function of reason to impose on itself. Humans are not governed only by Newtonian laws of physics, but are also self-governed, by laws which are the product of reason. If any human, or rational creature, acts out of a *desire* to bring something about, or from a motive such as lust or greed or even affection, then he acts as part of nature; he just does what it is inevitable that, as an animal, he would do, and no blame or credit attaches to him, any more than it attaches to another animal who acts in this way. It is only if he acts out of good will, that is a determination to do what it is his duty to do, according to the moral law he has rationally imposed upon himself, that his action is morally good, or indeed comes into the sphere of the moral at all. There exists in the world *nothing* morally good, according to Kant, except the good will. The rational law a man gives himself, when acting out of duty, or the good will, is the categorical imperative. In rational action, a man adopts a 'maxim', or stateable principle; and the primary form of the categorical imperative is to act only on that maxim which he could will to be a law governing not only his action here and now, but all actions of all people for ever, who were placed in the circumstances that he is placed in. Suppose a situation of shortage, say a drought; and suppose that there is a general ban on the use of hosepipes to water the garden. Now let us imagine that there is someone living in a remote house, with no spying neighbours, and sheltered by trees from any investigating helicopters. This person is about to enter his vegetables in a local show, and he longs to be able to water them. He realises that he could get away with it, and he is sorely tempted to use his hose. If all the same this person says to himself, 'It would be wrong to use my hose,' and feels strongly that he must not (perhaps his less morally conscientious wife is urging him to do so), this is because he cannot justify making an exception in his own favour. He cannot believe that everyone should use their hosepipes just as they wish, because this is contrary to the purpose of the ban: water would run out. What he wants is that he should use his hose, and not the others. But the categorical imperative, in other words his conscience, dictates that he *must* not, however much to his advantage it would be.

Such an analysis of the moral has much to recommend it. It seems to account for the sense we have that some things must or must not be done, regardless of our wishes; that there are principles that must be upheld everywhere and at all times, though the heavens fall; that whether or not you will be detected in wrong-doing, there are things you must not do, because they are intrinsically wrong. It seems in short to give sense to the idea of obligation, whether in the broad sense or in the narrow sense in which, for example, you can impose an obligation on yourself by promising. For if whether you kept a promise or not were allowed to depend on your wishes in the matter, then promises would become worthless. It is not enough to say to someone that you will meet their train, for example, and that you promise to be at the station, if this could be understood to mean that you would be there if and only if at the time you wanted to be there. If one breaks a promise one knows that it is wrong, and one knows also that one could not wish, or will, that everyone should do so. To break a promise is to ride on the back of an institution which in fact one wishes to continue. It is the same with lying. If there were no presumption in favour of truth-telling, if one did not know that one ought to tell the truth, and rely on other people to do so, in the main, then one could not get away with lying (and people who are known to be habitual liars are, in fact, excluded from the realm of ordinary, reliable truth-telling persons. Their words go generally unheeded.).

Kant held that it was reason that enabled people to impose such laws on themselves which would bind them inevitably, as the laws of logic bind one. There is a sense in which one *cannot* assert, for example, two contradictory predicates of the same subject (for instance that something has no colour and that it is green). Similarly, he argued, one *cannot* say that everyone must refrain from using their hosepipes in the garden and that, oneself, one may do so. It is a contradiction in the will. Of course people do make exceptions for themselves, and do things which they know they should not do. Kant was not particularly interested in the psychology of such immorality. All he wanted to do was to show, as he hoped, that it is profoundly irrational to act in a manner that is contrary to what you know is right, and this quite independently of any consequences, good or ill, that may flow from your doing so.

This bald outline of Kant's theory entirely fails to do justice to it as part of his whole grand critical design. For the main thread, running through all his critical philosophy, is his determination to reconcile the certainties of science, particularly of Newtonian physics, with a different certainty, that of the moral responsibilities of rational creatures. He held that in both scientific and everyday language, all that we can know is about how things appear to us. About the things themselves which lie behind these appearances, we can know nothing whatever, and any claims of metaphysics to tell us about the true nature of things, unmediated by our own perception of them, is nonsensical. The only exception to this is our awareness of our own freedom, either to obey or to disobey the moral law which, as rational creatures, we impose on ourselves, autonomously. Moral responsibility thus opens a chink of light into what is really the case as opposed to what appears to the eye of science to be the case. At the level of appearance, we, like all other objects in the world, are governed by physical laws. It is only the moral order which allows us to *know* that we exist otherwise than as appearances.

Detached, however, from Kant's all-embracing philosophical purpose, the doctrine of the categorical imperative will not really do, as an explanation of where ethics comes from. Its weakness lies in its separation of reason from all other human faculties and propensities. It may well be that it is reason which prevents our asserting, or at least believing, that something that is not coloured could, at the same time and with regard to the same aspect, be green. We doubtless feel that if we have inadvertently asserted these contradictory propositions, we *must* withdraw one of them. If we see a small child trying to put an object through a hole in a box lid, which will not go through, and then trying to put an even larger object through the same hole, we feel like saying to him, 'Come on, can't you *see* that if Y is larger than X and Z is larger than Y, then Z is larger than X?' It is not something we need to experiment to find out. We are debarred by logic from getting Z through the hole, if Y would not go through. Kant claims that in just the same way, we are debarred from using our hosepipe in the garden, while wishing that other people shall not use theirs. But of course we are not. We are perfectly capable of succumbing to temptation; the fear of contradicting ourselves, as far as our will goes, is not enough to prevent us. And he himself partly recognises this. Despite his insistence that to act morally well is to act according to a rational law, he also says that we act out of respect for, even awe of, the law of the categorical imperative. There is a grandeur in our ability to impose on ourselves duties which we must fulfil, though the heavens fall. It is awe or respect for this grandeur, the sense that we would be diminished if we did not obey the law, which in the end constrains us to obey. To act in accordance with duty thus becomes an ideal. To adopt an ideal is not and cannot be an entirely rational proceeding. It is to admire and to value something. In David Hume's words, 'What is honourable, what is fair, what is becoming, what is noble, what is generous, takes possession of the heart, and animates us to embrace and maintain it' (*An Enquiry concerning the Principles of Morals*, Book 1, section 1, para. 136). To refuse to turn on the hosepipe, despite the temptation to do so, is to show that you value the ideal of fairness, or non-cheating, more highly than you value winning the prize with your beans. You would be ashamed to win by cheating.

So what is shame? First, and most obviously, it is a social virtue. Although it is true that one may be ashamed all by oneself, indeed suffer agonies of shame, in the watches of the night, reflecting on what one did yesterday, it is always the thought of other people, what they did think, or what they would think if they knew, which constitutes the feeling. Sartre has a proof of the existence of other people, against the solipsist, which goes as follows: a man, in a rage of jealousy and suspicion, knows that his wife is in the drawing-room talking to, as he thinks, her lover. He is in the hall, alone, and he bends down to listen at the keyhole. While he is in this attitude, he hears a step behind him. Instantly he is transformed. Before, he was simply intent on what he wanted, on hearing the conversation the other side of the door. Now he has become an eavesdropper, seen as such by the other person in the hall. He is overcome by shame. Sartre uses this immediate transformation of the jealous man into an object, to be described and despised by someone else, as the proof that human beings cannot think of themselves as separate from other people, or as needing arguments to prove that other people exist: we are conscious of other people as part of all our consciousness. But the story can equally be used to show that shame (and many other emotions) is essentially experienced in a social context, where others are either actually or potentially present, and seeing us through other eyes than our own. The eavesdropper minds being caught in the act not because of the consequences his being caught may have (though it might have bad consequences), but here and now, without thought of the future, because he does not like to think of himself as mean, dishonourable, *low*. He despises such characteristics in others; and now he has to despise himself as well. This is what shame is.

However, this, though a step forward insofar as it points to a feeling which may be central in a moral context (and as we have seen Aristotle certainly thought that it was), does not yet define the moral. For one may feel shame if one has cause to despise oneself in contexts other than the moral. If I am an art historian, devoted not just to the ideal of sensibility, but to that of scholarship, and, in my excitement, am led to an ascription of a newly discovered painting which later turns out to be a forgery, I will feel ashamed of myself. I ought to have looked more closely, taken more care; I have lowered myself in my own eyes, as well as in the eyes of others. This is shame, but we still have not discovered the specifically moral nature of the shame which Sartre's man typically experiences.

Let us return to the idea of altruism, which, at the end of the last chapter, emerged as central to private, as opposed to public, morality. It is through a further exploration of this idea that the secret of the ethical may be discovered.

Since altruism is at the centre of my account of the ethical, it is necessary to make a bow towards, and then dismiss, the argument that there is no such thing as altruism, the putting of other people's interests before one's own. If, it is said, this appears to be what sometimes occurs, it is a matter of superficial appearance only (or perhaps of self-deception). In fact everyone pursues their own self-interest, and that alone. It is simply that some people like to pose as martyrs; they like the idea of sacrificing themselves for others; it is from this that they get satisfaction. So, in promoting the interests of others, they are really promoting their own. Now this is a difficult argument to refute, head-on. For if one uses the expressions 'to pursue one's own self-interest' or 'to seek one's own satisfaction' widely enough, then it might, uninterestingly, be said that this is what all motivation is: to do something because you want to do it. The only thing that would be excluded would be to do something because you were forced to. But obviously to use the expressions in this way is to make all motivation the same, and therefore all characters the same. Now if the subject-matter of ethics is people's characters and motives, and all characters and motives are the same, then there is really nothing to be said about ethics except that it is a delusion (to prove which is indeed the point of the argument against the possibility of altruism). If, however, like Aristotle and Kant, we start from where we are, from the phenomena, we find that there is a profound difference between the morally good and the morally bad, the ethical and the unethical, the nice person and the nasty person. As Hume put it, 'Let a man's insensibility be ever so great, he must often be touched with the images of Right and Wrong; and let his prejudices be ever so obstinate, he must observe that others are susceptible of like impressions. The only way, therefore, of converting an antagonist of this kind [one who denies the existence of ethics], is to leave him to himself ' (op. cit., para. 133). We simply cannot get on with the proposition that everyone is alike in these respects. The phenomena are too powerfully against it. We may therefore follow Hume's advice, and leave the antagonist alone. Let us put aside the suggestion that the distinctions are idle, that the differences do not really exist, and return to the way things are.

I shall try, in what follows, to state clearly what my convictions are about the nature of the ethical, and its origins. In forming these convictions, I have learned most from Aristotle, Hume and Kant, among 'classical' philosophers. Among modern philosophers, I have followed the arguments and insights especially of G.J. Warnock (*The Object of Morality*, Methuen, 1971) and David Wiggins (op. cit.). If I borrow from these philosophers, I shall not always acknowledge the debt, unless I quote their exact words. I suppose, also, that I have learned from my moralising nanny, and my pietistic school.

To be altruistic, then, is to be prepared to forgo what you might like to do, or to suppress a claim you might like to make for yourself, for the sake of other people. It is important to notice that, though sometimes your doing this may arise out of love or benevolence to those others (as when, in the war, many mothers gave up their share of extra or specially delicious food for their children), this is by no means essential to altruism. For besides such love, or special responsibility for some other individuals, human beings are linked to one another much more widely by sympathy, an imaginative understanding of other members of their species, based on what they have in common. Human imagination, expressed in human language, enables people to think and speak of things that are not in front of their eyes. Other animals, without imagination and language, can think only of what they can now perceive, or perhaps remember (though even when they remember, it seems that it requires some trigger to refresh their memory). We cannot suppose that animals, even the brightest of them, can deliberately recall or call up images of things unless reminded by something they see or hear or smell or, perhaps, dream. We use the very same language to describe ourselves as we use to describe others, whether we can see them or imagine or recall them. So if you know that *anyone* is starving, you can imagine what this is like, and you may be motivated therefore to give up something to remedy the ill. It is true that this link of sympathy is stronger when the others are close to us, literally or metaphorically, but because of the power we have, which is the power of imagination, to bring before our minds and hearts things that are not in our immediate vicinity, we can extend our sympathies, and feel the pains and pleasures of other people. J.S. Mill, wanting to argue both that each person desired his own pleasure and happiness, and also that to secure the pleasure and happiness of everyone is the goal of ethics, argued that if everyone wants his own happiness, it follows that the happiness of all is the goal of all. But there is a manifest sophistry here. Each one could go on all his life without ever thinking about the others. What Mill must have meant was that if each one did not raise his eyes from his own happiness to the happiness of others, there would be no such thing as ethics. If that was what he meant, then he was right. For each one to take on the needs, wishes, desires of others and make them into his goal is the beginning of the ethical. Because of his imagination, and his likeness to other people (expressed as sympathy), each one is capable of doing this, but to do it requires an *effort* of imagination and of sympathy. Altruism does not follow automatically from self-interest.

There is here, therefore, a possibility of conflict. In spite of imagination and the ability to experience sympathy with others, the human desire to further one's own interest and pursue one's own pleasure is extremely and often overwhelmingly strong. Children, for example, though they may be affectionate to others, tend to have no natural inclination to forgo what they want for the sake of what others want. (This is not always true. There are children with sweet unselfish natures, or so it seems, who naturally and without prompting want to share things.) The demands made on one by sympathy may thus very often be felt as themselves a source of conflict. They give rise to the feeling that what I want for myself is contrary to what my sympathy dictates. And this in turn gives rise to the feature of 'duty' insisted on by Kant, that it takes the form of a command, not an inclination. It is because a person who has embarked on an ethical career of altruism knows that the world would be better, and he would be better, if his sympathies were not so limited and so lacking in force, compared with his own wishes for himself, that he will say that he must act for the good of another, against his inclination and in obedience to the dictates of 'stern duty'.

There are two cautions to add, for the sake of clarity. Things would go, on the whole, better if we could extend our sympathies to all who suffer, and feel the need to make things better for them, treating them as our brothers. Yet it can be argued that the further we extend our sympathy, the further we extend the sphere of our duties, or what we *ought* to do; and it would be impossible to fulfil duties universally. It is a maxim often repeated by moral philosophers, that 'ought implies can'. You cannot be under an obligation to do what it is impossible for you to do. I do not wholly subscribe to this maxim. For sometimes our keenest *feeling* of moral obligation arises with regard to things we cannot do, either because the opportunity to do them has passed, or because we are otherwise prevented from fulfilling them. Nevertheless I believe it is true that one could not have an absolutely unlimited duty. Moreover to concentrate too much on the width rather than the depth of our human sympathies may lead not only to absurdly impossible duties, but to the neglect of duties which we can and must fulfil, which are truly binding, and which are nearer home. It may sometimes seem that it would be better, for example, in the teaching of schoolchildren to concentrate less on the moral evils of destroying rain forests, and more on the close-to-home evils of bullying or stealing. This is not, however, to alter the central point that it is the imaginative conception of the needs and wishes of others besides oneself, the sense of them as important, to which we have given the name of sympathy, which is the source of ethics.

The second caution is this. We should distinguish between sympathy and a kind of universal benevolence or beneficence. In the *Treatise of Human Nature*, Hume denied that there is any such thing as a perfectly general benevolence towards mankind as a whole. He gave various elaborate accounts of the mechanism by which sympathy could arouse passions in us, a desire to mitigate the pains or share in the pleasures of others, but such sympathy did not amount to general benevolence. It had to be activated afresh with every bit of news we got, so to speak, of the experiences of others. Fifteen years later, when he published the *Enquiry concerning the Principles of Morals*, he had changed his mind, and argued that morality was founded on such general benevolence, though not on this alone. It seems to me plain, however, that if there were someone with an absolutely general wish to do good to people, in every situation, this would run counter to what we think of as morally good behaviour. For in each situation in which he found himself, this person would have to work out what would in fact most benefit his fellow human beings. The first sufferer would be justice. It might well be that, the laws being as they are, a murder has plainly been committed, and the murderer convicted. Yet the person murdered might be a drug-pushing child-molester, who had caused nothing but harm, the murderer a young married man with a job, for whom life imprisonment would be a disaster. The judge and jury might feel positive benevolence towards the murderer. But their benevolence must not go too far, or justice would be undermined. The laws of private property cannot be suspended because hundreds of ramblers would enjoy walking over the moors without restriction. And though it is doubtless true that a general desire to do good rather than harm, universally, is the sign of an amiable person, yet if this were a person's only consideration, he might be at least unreliable, when it came, for example, to fulfilling promises, doing what he was hired to do, generally acting in obedience to what he conceived to be harmful laws. In each case, he would find himself overriding his obvious obligation by the consideration that more good would come to more people if he did something different. Though general benevolence is doubtless preferable, and morally preferable, to general malevolence, it seems plain that it cannot be the sole foundation of the ethical.

The ethical, then, arises when someone begins to see that he must postpone his immediate wishes for the sake of the good. And 'the good' here embraces both his own goodness, and the goodness of the society of which he is a member. It arises, to lapse into metaphor, when people begin to see that, first their own society, then human beings at large are all in the same boat, and it is a precarious boat that will sink if there is no co-operation among those who are on board. Thus arises a willingness to be generous, to share, to restrain one's natural wishes when their fulfilment would damage the rest of the boat-load. In a precarious situation, people must assert and share certain values, or perish. It is this realisation, it seems to me, which lies at the root of the ethical. This is what opens up the possibility of altruism, as each person thinks for himself, about his own relation to the rest.

Within society, the criminal laws are there only to restrain the behaviour of those who have developed no intrinsic sense of the moral in particular areas of their lives, no general sense of responsibility to other people, based on sympathy. But behind the criminal law lie principles, such as a principle of protecting life, or promise-keeping or truth-telling, which are values *to be relied on* by all members of society. And these principles give rise not just to the law, but to the sense of personal obligation apart from the law which Kant placed at the centre of his moral theory, and which we have seen may make us feel constrained to postpone our own interests to the interests of others, or of society at large.

However, such principles and their consequent obligations are not all we have to use. We can, after all, love and admire people (our fellow passengers on the boat) for many virtues, for courage, truthfulness, clear-headedness, amiability, sheer niceness, as well as for adherence to principles. And it is such admiration that allows us to embrace ideals, and thus to think imaginatively about the kind of persons we would like to be. We make our distinctions with regard to people's characters according to whether they possess these various virtues or their opposite vices. We examine our own motives to see whether they arise from or at least are consistent with a character of which we should not be ashamed. Such is the collection of concepts (not just one) from which the idea of the ethical is born. The concepts are not always in harmony with one another. The clear-headed person may be cruel; the courageous person may go head-on for a destructive policy. But the fundamental virtues are those which lead to co-operation; and for the sake of co-operation my own wishes may have to go by the board. This is the sense in which I believe that altruism is central to private morality. And without the private motive to behave ethically well, the public ethics, directed to the common good, would founder.

Finally, it is perhaps just worth reiterating that though this may look like a semi-historical account of where ethics came from, it is not truly historical. It is rather an attempted account of what ethics *is*. However it is not a static account. We can read Aristotle and see how his analysis of practical reason, his description of the virtues, his belief in the possibility of ethical education fits with what ethics is. Yet he had no word for duty, or for conscience. He had no idea of those specifically Christian virtues, charity and humility, even sincerity. The scene changes, but ethics remains recognisably the same, because the need for an ethical system is a fundamental need of human nature.

Freedom, Responsibility and Determinism

As we saw in the last chapter, those who deny the possibility of altruism deny that the subject-matter of ethics exists; for they deny any difference in motivation between the morally good person who is at least *prepared* to sacrifice his own interest to the interest of others, and the morally evil. All alike, they allege, act in pursuit of their own satisfaction. There is another way in which, notoriously, the real existence of ethics may seem to be denied, and that is the theory that choice itself is illusory: everything we do or think is determined in advance, and we have no way of influencing the situation we are in, through choosing what to do or to refrain from. At no time ever is it true to say that we could have acted otherwise than we did. It is necessary, quite briefly, to consider at least some versions of this theory, and to dispose of it, if our guide is not to lead, after all, into a dead-end. So this will be an almost entirely theoretical chapter, necessary before the drawing of any general practical conclusions out of what has gone before.

The apparent incompatibility of ethics and determinism is held to arise in the following way. Ethics is concerned with our attitudes towards people's behaviour. We admire and despise, praise and blame, punish and sometimes reward people for what they do on purpose, deliberately or by their own choice. If we believe that they could not but behave in the way they did, then we put them outside the scope of these specifically ethical attitudes. So if it were to be shown that they could not help anything at all, that they are on tram-lines, inexorably causing them to travel the way they are travelling, turning at each cross-road the way the lines take them, then, it is said, ethics would disappear, and our ethical vocabulary would become redundant, or at least, if used, would have to take on quite new meanings. We might, for example, praise people for the usefulness of their behaviour, or for their elegance or wit, but without ascribing any *moral* merit to them for being as they are, just as we speak of animals other than humans. Of these, we admire some and dislike others, without thereby ascribing to them any ethical qualities at all. A fault in a non-human animal cannot be a moral fault.

It is sometimes alleged by determinists that there would still be a use for ethical language and ethical judgement, even if determinism were shown to be true. For just as with other animals, we might find that people could be trained to act differently by praise or blame, or by being punished. This praise and blame would no longer be *deserved*, in the sense in which we normally understand this term, for it would not be accorded to anything which someone had, after reflection, deliberately chosen to do, when they might have done something else; yet we might simply find that shouting at them, or saying that they had been wicked, or locking them up in consequence of their behaviour, actually worked, in practice, to deter either them or others. Manifesting disapproval of, or rewarding, people would be a way of to some extent altering the direction of the tram-lines they were running along. It would say nothing about the moral worth of the person. Such a view of the language of morals has been proposed, though I believe that in practice it would be difficult to use either consistently or with real conviction. Moreover it seems to depend on the rather disagreeable view that the people who do the punishing or rewarding know that what they are doing is without grounds and without justice; whereas the people who are the recipients of such abuse or praise are not in the know; they are suckers, taken in by the apparent authority of these verbal or other inter-changes, and continuing to believe that they are to blame when they are not, or have merited praise or reward when that has been offered. I am reminded of a visit I once paid to a school for severely disabled children in New York which was devoted to behaviour modification as a method of teaching. I was told at the beginning of the day that none of the children could understand what was meant by doing well or badly, or trying to do better, but that they responded to reward if they succeeded and punishment if they failed. The rewards took the form of Smarties (or the American equivalent); the punishment took the form of a hostile tone of voice, and a mild slap. After a regime of this kind, continued for several weeks, I was told, the children's performance of specific tasks tended to improve. This was the theory. I did not look forward to witnessing this inhuman-sounding process; but I need not have worried. There was a child, recently arrived at the school, who was being taught the co-ordination needed to wheel a large rubber tyre across the room. The teacher helped her perform the task, which she found impossibly demanding. But she was never spoken to roughly, let alone slapped. At the end of her first, disastrous, attempts she was handed a lot of Smarties, and told she had been wonderful; she had really tried. The teacher turned to me and said, 'Isn't Lizzie doing well? She came to us only yesterday. You are doing brilliantly, Lizzie.' And so on. The teacher was too human and too loving to do anything except hand out praise, and encouragement to effort, and she made no attempt to divest her words of their ordinary meanings nor to show a negative reaction to failure. I believe that this defence of the continued use of ethical concepts, if determinism is true, is futile because impossible, and I shall say no more about it.

However, I want now to defend in a different way the common-sense view that there really is a subject-matter for ethics, by seeking to show that even the scientists among us need not accept determinism, or the total predictability of human behaviour, as a fact. The problem of freedom and determinism, or 'predestination', is of great antiquity. Milton in *Paradise Lost* represents the angels in

heaven as discussing free will and 'foreknowledge absolute'; and this was indeed one of the early forms that the
problem took, in Christian thought. How could God be
omniscient if He did not know precisely what you would
do; and how could He know this, and it still be true that
you freely chose what to do, and might have done something different? The essence of the problem, then as now,
was predictability. We want to be, not random in our
conduct, but to a certain extent *unpredictable*. We want to
be able to claim to have made, for example, a difficult
choice; to have withstood a temptation to which we might
have succumbed; to have decided on our own to take a
course, even if that course turned out in the end to be
disastrous.

And so by far the most usual version of determinism
in modern times has been the supposed determinism of
science, and especially of physics. After Newton, physics
was the science which seemed to promise both a fundamental account of the composition of the world, and laws
which, if pursued far enough, should render every event
predictable. We have seen how Kant sought to get out of
the difficulty; all of the natural world is governed by the
laws of Newtonian physics, and this goes for human
beings as well, *except* insofar as they are rational creatures, able to make laws for themselves, and to choose, on
pain of self-contradiction, to obey them. This rationality
is real freedom. But we have also seen the limitations of
Kant's theory, magnificent though it is. For to adopt it
would entail the belief that human beings are free only if

and when they are acting in obedience to the moral law. For most of their lives, indeed for all of their lives except when faced with a crisis of conscience, they would be as much subject to the laws of the natural sciences as other objects in the world, their actions, beliefs, affections, reactions as predictable in principle as the movements of the planets. And this limited freedom is not what we want to assert. We want to be as free to decide whether to have a boiled egg or a scrambled egg for our supper as to decide whether to lie to get out of a difficulty, or keep a promise which it does not suit us to keep. All choices must be free, not just a few morally significant choices. If everyday and trivial choices were wholly predictable by scientific laws, even if predicting might in practice be difficult, then all choices would be so predictable. We have found no inducement to follow Kant along the path of total separation between reason and other aspects of human life; nor do moral choices seem to be uniquely and entirely the function of reason. Nice people make ethically better choices than nasty people, something which Kant could not allow.

Since Newton, then, determinism has taken the form of a commitment to the scientific view of the world, within which every event has a cause, even though that cause might not yet have been discovered. And if humans are objects in the world, as they plainly are, then their behaviour must, in principle, be subject like all other objects to causal explanations. There is no room for choice, or unpredictability.

Before tackling this argument directly, it is perhaps

right to get out of the way certain other supposed threats to human freedom, which have arisen mainly in the last century. These are threats from a kind of determinism based on the social as opposed to the physical sciences, especially psychology and economics. For example, Freud's theory of unconscious motivation has sometimes been held to show the unreality of conscious choice. We are held by this theory to be conditioned entirely by our past experiences, and thereafter to make choices not according to the reasons we would allege, but according to non-rational motives which arise out of this past. It was to combat some such determinism as this that Sartre insisted that the past does not exist as a power to dictate what we choose to do. We invent our own pasts, to suit our present book; and, in the present, every choice is open to us, if only we will face facts. But we fear freedom, and therefore seek to deny it, and fall back, in bad faith, on saying that our character has been fixed in our past. Sartre later repudiated the extreme simplicity of his original position, that human beings can choose absolutely anything, without any restrictions imposed on them by their own history (a position perhaps influenced by his desire to encourage a belief in their own limitless freedom among those overtly bound by the Occupation of France). Nevertheless, in an interview in 1969, he still asserted that 'the idea I have never ceased to develop is that in the end one is always responsible for what is made of one. Even if one can do nothing else besides assume this responsibility. For I believe that a man can always make something out of what is made of him.' In any case Freudian determinism seems never to have been a radical determinism. For the theory, in at least some of its versions, is that once I recognise unconscious purposes which have rendered me a slave to my neurosis, I shall be able to step out from them, free as air.

Sartre had a more intractable problem when, after 1945, he took up Marxism. For Marxists claimed to explain and to predict all human conduct in terms of the economic factors within which a person might live and work. And they claimed further that such explanations were wholly material: there was no place in them for wishes, wants, intentions. There were economic needs which drove people collectively to certain standard forms of conduct. Sartre accepted this theory as an account of the history of mankind, but sought to conjoin it with the existentialist view of each individual, looking out from behind his own eyes and seeing the world as a field for his own choices, for shaping his own life. The last books that Sartre wrote (of enormous length) were all devoted to the attempted solution of this problem, as well as the problem of psychological determinism. He settled for a bold theory that individuals made their own 'projects' of how to live their lives, but these projects, when carried into effect, actually changed the material and economic world in which they lived. Therefore it was only through the biography of individuals told in total detail that one could see the relation between a person's choices and the way his environment impinged on him. Through a biography which told everything you could tell the story, not only of the man, but of the historically determined arena within which he lived and fought his individual battles, and to which his particular choices contributed. The trouble with this theory was that it was impossible to prove that, in the end, individual choices *could* exist alongside historical inevitability or that the biographer's language, purporting to reveal the inner life of the subject, was *really* compatible with materialism. The attempt to reconcile even a limited individual freedom with a full-blown theory of historical-economic inevitability cannot be said to have been a success (though it is hard to tell whether it was or not: for Sartre's writing had by now become excessively repetitive, long-winded and obscure).

In any case, the problem of incompatibility between the social sciences version of determinism and a belief in the free choices of the individual to the solution of which Sartre directed his energies seems to be more apparent than real. There is no justification for economics or psychology or indeed sociology asserting an absolute law-like regularity within their particular subject-matter. None of these supposed sciences has had much success in predicting how the future will be, based on discoveries of how things are. It seems to me that it was only their pretensions to be sciences, to model themselves on the natural sciences, which ever made it seem possible to claim that they could explain everything, including human choices.

And so we come back to the old threat to freedom: the

threat of the natural sciences. Is all choice (and therefore all moral choice, and the existence of moral subject-matter) a delusion? Can the whole world, including the human world, be described in terms of physical laws, which make one thing, including one human action, in principle deducible from that which went before? The form that these questions take has, naturally, changed since Kant confronted Newtonian physics. But in essence the problem is the same. The natural sciences seem to be based on the assumption that every event occurs as a result of some preceding set of events. And what these preceding events or causes are can in principle be discovered. If an event is caused, it is causally determined. That and only that which occurs could have occurred, given the antecedent circumstances. Everything you or I or anyone does, however much we think we are choosing, is predictable, or would be predictable, if only we knew more. Freedom is nothing but ignorance of necessity.

There is very little inclination these days for those who want to assert that the will is free to suggest that there is a completely different set of activities which are entirely distinct from physical goings-on, and which are autonomous. No one is much inclined to think of 'reason' or 'volition' as separate from the physical world, the Ghost in the Machine. This great change has come about because of the development of and quite remarkable interest in the science of neurophysiology. We are, I believe, liberated at last from Cartesian dualism, according to which the mind is thought of as a different substance altogether from the body. We know that we think and decide with our brains, and that in this respect we are like all other animals, only brighter. And we know that our brains are physical objects different from, but no less physical than, tables and chairs, and computers. And finally we believe that for every thought or wish or feeling that we experience, there is some correlated brain state, which could, in principle, be separately identified. Now if we add to these beliefs a further belief, that every brain state is brought into being, causally, by a preceding brain state, then it seems that physical (or physiological) determinism is inevitable, and that all our wishes, desires and choices, and therefore all our behaviour, could be predicted, if we knew the laws which governed the causing of one brain state by another. We could then dispense with the whole vocabulary of the 'inner life', and therefore, obviously, with the vocabulary of ethics, as we currently understand it. Our intentions or motives, which are held to distinguish between what is good in our behaviour and character and what is bad, would be of no further interest. A very accurate and precise encephalograph attached to my head, and read off by you, would tell you what I was going to do, and enable you, according to the relevant causal laws, to predict my future, as well as know my present actions. (Such views are set out, for example, in an essay by Ted Honderich, entitled 'One Determinism' in *Philosophy As It Is* edited by Honderich and Burnyeat, Pelican, 1979.)

Although today hardly anyone would deny that human beings and their brains are physical objects in a world of physical objects, the crucial question remains whether causal laws could, even 'in principle' (that useful defensive phrase), be found which could predict in detail how events in a brain could be translated, causally, into actions of an individual.

On the one hand there are those who think of a brain as a computer, and therefore such that, given a certain input, a certain regular output in the form of action or reaction is to be relied on. The adding to the computer brain of a robot 'body' actually to make the relevant movements seems a relatively minor extra. These are philosophers interested in the concept of artificial intelligence, who believe that there is no limit to the extent that a computer could be constructed which would perform all the tasks that a human can; not just tasks such as solving chess problems, but those demanding decision-making in less restricted and obviously rule-governed circumstances than a game. Moreover, while many of those interested in developing artificial intelligence believe that a computer could be made which would *model* everything the brain did, there are others who would go further, and argue that the brain *is* a computer, its functions wholly describable from outside it, in terms of inputs and outputs, so that the very concept of first-person experience (including of course the experience of trying to make up one's mind, or coming to a decision) will be seen to be redundant. On the other hand, there are those, among whom I am one, who hold that these philosophers have overlooked the crucial and obvious difference between the biological and the physical sciences.

I am not a scientist of any kind, biological or physical; yet I can understand, I think, the following picture. Within the brain of every animal there is the ability to identify and reidentify kinds of objects which are significant for it, which, for it, have a value. It is this recognition of things to be pursued or avoided that is essential to the survival of an animal. It is not just rats running in mazes in the laboratory which learn the way to the food, or how to avoid the electric shocks they will get if they take one route rather than another. They can do these things because animals all do them in the wild (though not many as cleverly as rats). Even such, to us, lowly creatures as flat-worms or octopuses have the ability to value things and learn to pursue or avoid them. They select from their environment the stimuli that are significant, and each animal learns to do this as it develops, in accordance with the Darwinian development of the species. But of course the actual stimuli that come to each individual animal may be different from those which come to the rest. If we consider a flock of goldfinches, suddenly descending on a garden, and hopping, fluttering, on all the bushes, we know that there is a large number of individual goldfinches, though we are not especially interested in distinguishing one from another. Do we think that the behaviour of each is determined? Well, probably we would agree that they are all after the same thing, the buds or seeds on the bushes; and we would probably agree that goldfinches inherit, in their genes, the ability to recognise the food that is palatable to them. But it is still open to us to ask what makes one individual bird flutter at just this moment, and another decide it has had enough, and lead the whole flock away. We presume, if we think about it, that it has been perceptual inputs that brought the birds into the garden, and perceptual inputs that finally lead them out. But, descending to the particular, was the behaviour of each individual bird *predictable*? Is there a law, or could a law be discovered, that would enable one to map out in advance the behaviour of the individuals in the flock, as soon as they arrived? I would say that this is extremely unlikely. For it would be impossible to predict exactly what and when each bird would perceive a significant object and seek it or avoid it. If my cat comes into the garden, it must be uncertain, in advance, which bird will be the first to spot it, and start the flight away. The brains of animals are not fixed like computers. They themselves change as circumstances change. The distinction between hardware and software, essential to computers, does not work with living creatures. Gerald Edelman, in his book *Bright Air, Brilliant Fire* (Basic Books, 1992), argues that the brain is a system analogous to the immune system, which, when it is working properly, forms antibodies even when quite unexpected and new viruses enter the body. In such a way the brain develops ways of adapting to new events. Each animal, even within one species, has its own selective and adaptational system, depending on what actually happens to it during its life.

Thus, in contrast with a physical theory of the brain, a biological theory has the advantage of showing that each individual human being is unique. It is true that the species, *Homo sapiens*, has evolved over the centuries to reach the position it has, with primary consciousness such as other animals have, the anatomical capacity to articulate a complicated and diverse language and the sort of higher consciousness which probably develops as language itself develops. But each member of the species develops its own awareness of the world and its own value system, restricted only by the genes it has inherited. To quote Edelman (op. cit., p. 82), 'The individuality and structural diversity of brains even within one species is confounding to models that consider the brain to be a computer. Evidence from developmental studies suggests that the extraordinary diversity at the finest ramifications of neural networks is an unavoidable consequence of the embryological process. That degree of diversity could not be tolerated in a computer system, following instructions.'

From the point of view of one wishing to question determinism, the crucial point of the biological account of the brain is the fact that at the embryonic stage the neurons in the brain move about in huge numbers until they finally settle in their places on other cells. And unlike any other object, the brain organises itself, that is to say, the cells move about and interconnect in unpredictable ways. The system is statistically variable. Though there is broad similarity between the arrangement of cells within the brains of members of the same species, there is not uniformity. This means that predictability is not merely difficult (which everyone would agree), it is in principle impossible. The development of neurophysiology has thus made the spectre of total predictability of human behaviour in terms of physical laws recede, if not completely vanish. It is open to us now to say simply that determinism, within the subject-matter of biology, is not true.

Nevertheless, there has arisen, in the last decade or so, what has seemed to many people a new threat to the concept of free choice, and the possibility of ethics, and this is the concept of genetic engineering. For my part, I do not believe that there is really a new kind of determinism entailed in this possibility. We have known, ever since the discovery of DNA, how genetics links one generation with another, what the mechanism is for the inheritance of characteristics from parents to child. Long before this discovery, of course, it was known to common sense as well as to science that children inherit characteristics, abilities, or proneness to certain diseases from their ancestors. That certain traits run in families is by no means a new idea. What is new is the belief that, because of our ever-increasing understanding of the details of the human genome, and the possibility of 'mapping' the genome of each individual, we shall in future be able to intervene, either to eliminate certain unwanted genetically inherited conditions, or, more speculatively, to cause, in a new generation of children, certain wanted and desirable characteristics, by replacing one gene by another.

The first thing to say about this belief (or fear) is that it presupposes another belief, which is that a person's genes determine, in important and predictable respects, what they will be like, and thus what they will do. And this, like any deterministic belief, would entail that whatever people are like, whatever they do, we should not be able to ascribe to them responsibility, moral merit or demerit. Whatever they do, it is as a result of the genes that they inherit. The *new* fear is that not only will people act as their genes 'make' them act, but that other people, parents, perhaps, or the medical profession, will be able to decide in what way they are 'made' to behave.

But the argument of the previous paragraphs should be enough to show that this presupposition is unfounded. A human being (or any other animal or plant) certainly inherits genes, and the future of that animal or plant is *in part* determined by the genes it inherits. But even in the case of plants, and still more of animals, the difference between one individual and another will also in part be determined by the environment within which the living organism grows. In the case of humans, as we have seen, the embryonic development of each is different, the arrangement of cells in the brain unpredictable. And since the environment of each human, the input through the senses, is different, so the development of each individual is unique. Our genetic inheritance, that is to say, may provide a framework, which limits the directions within which we shall develop. But such limitations are not like tram-lines. The brain itself changes over time, and so does its reaction to its peculiar environment. Since no two people, even no two identical twins, are exactly alike in the manner in which their brains develop and react, we have no reason to suppose that, even with the most extensive and exact knowledge of the genome of each, we would be able to predict what they would do, or what they would make of their environment. And we can no more predict, in detail, the changing features of their environment than we could predict exactly what would move the individual goldfinches in our flock to flutter this way or that way.

It may still be suggested that what I am saying amounts only to this, that it is very difficult to predict what people will do; but that if we knew more, we could do so: people's behaviour may not be determined by their genes alone, but by their genes and their environment together, and this in principle could be known. But this is the precise opposite of what I am saying. I am asserting that the reaction of an individual to the infinite variety of his environment is unpredictable, in principle. We could not form a deterministic account of the future of any living animal. In the case of human animals, the impossibility is compounded by that unique feature of humans, their imagination. For humans, and they alone, are able not only to learn from their past experiences (as all animals can) but consciously to envisage a future for themselves which may differ from the past. They are able not only to pursue the things they have learned to value highly and avoid those they have learned to hate (as laboratory rats do), but they can form pictures for themselves of the universe as a whole and the part they would wish to play in it. They can give themselves goals to pursue, which may be totally new and idiosyncratic, or which they have learned from people they have, unpredictably, met or read about, admired or loved. It is this ability to set new goals, newly invented or traditional, but, either way, taken on individually by the unique human being, which lies at the root of ethics, and remains untouched by the genetic inheritance each may have. And this remains true even if, improbably, we should try to change that genetic inheritance by gene therapy or gene manipulation. I say 'improbably' because, although I think and hope that genetic manipulation may become a reality, insofar as the replacement of one identified faulty gene could eliminate a particular disease which is the result of one 'rogue' gene only (a monogenetic disease such as cystic fibrosis, or Duchenne's muscular dystrophy), it seems in the last degree unlikely that single genes or even combinations of genes could be found which would make a child brave or public-spirited or generous. Such descriptions as these reflect the general way in which a human being reacts to his environment. But if each individual is unique, and his environment, in detail, unpredictable, there could never be any certainty, in the case of an individual, that the intervention would 'work' to have the desired effect.

Education is more likely to succeed in such matters than genetic manipulation.

I do not believe, then, that the possibility of genetic manipulation should be regarded as a new threat to human freedom. People who think that it is are expressing a new and sophisticated version of an old fear, that science is incompatible with freedom. But I hope to have suggested that, whatever might have been true of the uniformities supposed to belong to Newtonian physics, biology, the science of living organisms, carries no such threat. And biology must be regarded as a different system of knowledge, irreducible, by the very nature of its subject-matter, to the science of physics.

So far, I have mostly addressed the problem of determinism and its incompatibility with freedom in the traditional way; and I have argued that, as far as living creatures go, determinism, if this entails predictability, cannot exist. To the extent, then, that this argument is acceptable, freedom is secured, and with it the possibility of ethics. However, there is a different place to start, and that is, in the manner of Aristotle and Kant, from the phenomena. In this last part of the chapter I want to go back, briefly, to the teacher who apparently could not use the language of ethics without its old meanings, who could not, in practice, follow the programme of behaviour modification. Here I am indebted (as everyone must be who considers the problem of freedom) to Sir Peter Strawson's British Academy Lecture of 1962, *Freedom and Resentment*.

We should not be blinded, or cowed, by the belief that there is one and only one kind of explanation for behaviour, the causal. If we start from where we are, we can see that science is only one among human activities, and the supposed causal, law-like explanations which science seeks (although, as I hope to have shown, it cannot always find them) are not the only kind of explanations. Equally important, indeed more important for most people, are explanations not of objective features of the universe, but of what may be called 'subjective' phenomena, the events of people's inner life. By this I mean the kind of explanations we give and accept of why people *feel* as they do, or why they act from the motives they act from. This kind of explanation, incidentally, relies to a certain extent on our own understanding of the way we feel ourselves, and why we do so; but our own feelings and states of mind are necessarily such that they are to be expressed in a common language, which in turn entails that they can be ascribed to other people besides ourselves. If I say of someone else that he is motivated by jealousy, I use the word 'jealousy' in exactly the same sense as I use it to express jealous feelings in myself. There is not a first-person sense of 'jealous' distinct from a third-person sense. This fact is the necessary condition of sympathy, central to the very existence of ethics.

Strawson, in his lecture, starts from the phenomenon of our reactive attitudes towards other people; and he takes resentment as a typical case. I resent it if someone displays ill-will towards me, or is totally careless of my interests. I resent it, for example, if someone deliberately treads on my toe. The pain may be the same, if someone accidentally treads on my toe in the course of trying to help me, or is caused, by the press of a crowd, inadvertently to tread on my toe. But in the latter cases I do not resent it; resentment is a natural reaction only in cases where I think that the agent need not have acted as he did. There is an enormous range of such natural reactions, to feel which is to show that we have a framework of interactions with other humans, whom we regard as inevitably linked with ourselves, insofar as they too will react to us in intelligible ways.

Besides these personal and immediate reactions, Strawson argues that there exist more generalised reactions, where I may feel not resentment against some individual who has injured me personally, but moral indignation or disapproval, where someone else has been injured, or where, though it is in fact I who have been injured, I believe other people would suffer injury from this *kind* of behaviour. And this, he argues, is the ethical reaction. (Of course this distinction may be difficult to draw in practice. It is easy for me to deceive myself that it is my ethical principles that have been outraged, when in fact all I am suffering from is a sense of personal affront, or a desire for 'compensation' for an injury: think of the people who demand compensation for, say, the death of a child on the self-righteous grounds that all they want is to ensure that other people do not suffer in the same way.) The phenomenon from which we start, then, is this: we treat people as capable of acting responsibly, and making deliberate choices, and our spontaneous attitudes towards them *entail* that we do so. We are able, in specific cases, to exempt them from responsibility, either because what they did was an accident, or a pardonable mistake; or because we think they themselves are not capable of responsibility, not yet, say, because they are children, or no longer, because they are suffering from senile dementia. The immediate and personal reactive attitude is connected with the more general, or moral, attitude, and they are linked through sympathy. Our personal resentment blossoms out, through sympathy, and may spread to others than ourselves.

Our sentiments towards other responsible people (including of course not just resentment and moral disapprobation, but gratitude and love and admiration), and their attitudes to us, are of central importance to our lives. The question is whether we can conceive of living, as a human being among other human beings, without these attitudes and reactions. It is obviously possible, as I have said, to exempt people for various reasons from responsibility, because they are not the sort of people who can be held responsible. But so to exempt them is to exclude them from the universe of moral sentiments, in the way that other animals are excluded. These are people with whom we cannot fully interact. The question then is could we treat everyone so? And could we conceivably be persuaded that we must so treat them by a *theory*, say, that all of everybody's actions are predictable according to laws governing the physical structures of their brains?

It seems to me self-evident that we could not, and remain ourselves human. There may be human beings who regard their fellow humans as no different from other things in the world, simply as objects to be used, avoided, manipulated, even disposed of as other things are. But we would normally say of such people that they are psychopaths, lacking altogether both human affections and moral sense. Psychopaths are notoriously among those whom we cannot ourselves treat as fully human; that is we know that we cannot interact normally with them, nor they with us. And thus they are among those exempted. But it is logically impossible that everyone should be so treated. The psychopath is abnormal, and this is not a state that everyone could be in.

We are disconcerted when we realise that other people treat us as unable to do things which we believe we can do if we try. Sartre has a chilling story in which a habitually unpunctual man turns up late yet again at the office, and tells his boss that he would have been in time, he could have been in time, only it so happened, just this once, that his car wouldn't start. He will be in time tomorrow. His boss says, 'It may be so. I should like to believe you.' The boss figure is treating his employee as simply the object of inductive reasoning, as one might treat a faulty piece of machinery. It is not absolutely impossible that it will right itself, but we base our certainty that it won't on past experience. A promise, in such a case, means nothing.

When we are thus treated as an object, like a bit of machinery, even though *we* still think we are free, it changes our position in the world. We become inhuman.

I take it then that Strawson's argument, far more detailed and subtle than the bits of it I have borrowed, leads to the conclusion that physical determinism is irrelevant to the facts of human freedom and responsibility, involved in our life of interpersonal attitudes. Biological determinism, even if it existed, would have no better a claim. We can forget the question whether we are free or determined. In real life, starting from the phenomena, what we do know is that our immediate and our more generalised reactions to people commit us to a belief in personal responsibility, and thus to ethics.

What Follows?

So much, or almost so much, for theory. In this final chapter I want to try to show in more practical terms that ethics is not only possible, but essential to our lives; how disrupted, anarchical and impoverished life would be if the centrality of ethics were denied, or the need, quite often, to adopt an ethical point of view were obscured. Ethical theory, however, cannot be entirely removed from this demonstration. The point of a Guide is rather to show how theory and practice interlock.

If I seem unduly intolerant or minatory in what follows it is because, given the nature of the subject-matter, one's feelings must be engaged. Hume remarked that matters of morality were more properly 'felt than judged of'. He modified this, by insisting that it was only a specific kind of feeling that counted in moral judgements: ''Tis only when a character is considered in general, without reference to our particular interest, that it causes such a feeling or sentiment as denominates it morally good or evil' (*A Treatise of Human Nature*, Book III, part 1, section 2), yet he was surely also right to suggest that without feeling, or sentiment, there could be no moral judgement at all. If to judge something morally wrong were simply to judge that it would have undesirable or harmful consequences, then there would be no difference between saying that something was wrong and saying that it was inexpedient. Yet there is a difference. The proper reaction to a moral wrong is indignation or outrage; and these reactions are essentially matters of sentiment (in the eighteenth-century meaning of the term) not of reason or calculation alone. The subject-matter of ethics demands that one become emotionally as well as theoretically and philosophically committed to one's beliefs.

Ethics, or morality, derives from certain incontrovertible *facts* about human beings and their difference from other animals; and among these is the fact that humans alone have developed an awareness of their own position in the world, and an ability to think of the past and future, as well as the present, the absent as well as what is in front of their eyes, what they would like to be as well as what they are. Along with this goes the ability to communicate with other people, in language. These abilities can be referred to collectively as human imagination. Because they are possessed of imagination, human beings cannot but be aware that their life is precarious, difficult and far from perfect. They are conscious of the *peccata mundi*, not sins, so much as intrinsic flaws in the world, including flaws in themselves. We are all prone to follow too much the desires of our own hearts, our own selfish wishes; and our sympathy with others, though it exists as part of our imaginative nature, is limited, both by selfishness and by *failures* of imagination. We are therefore subject to temptation, the temptation to pursue the narrow goals of self-interest, forgetful of the equal needs and wishes of other people, especially if these others are not our immediate family or friends. As soon as we recognise the fact of temptation, and of limited imagination, even sporadically, we have adopted the ethical point of view. It is part of that same viewpoint to believe ourselves to be free to try to overcome such temptations and limitations, to give ourselves new goals to aim for, and to adopt *ideals* towards which we can strive. For, as we have seen, if we are not in some sense free, ethics ceases to be a possibility. Moral decisions are an illusion.

It will be noticed, perhaps with irritation, that I constantly use the word 'we' in defining the ethical point of view; and this is inevitable. Human beings are necessarily members of a society, however loosely structured. They must therefore think of themselves as essentially plural; and indeed if this were not so the question of ethics, of what ought to be done, would hardly arise except in a wholly instrumental sense (what ought I to do, if I am to be rescued from my desert island?). For, however desperate and apparently unique one's personal dilemma, to ask, in an ethical sense, 'What am I to do?' can always be, more or less, translated into the question 'What is *one* to do?' If I finally decide what it would be right to do, then I must be able to justify my decision that it was right in general terms. Indeed, to think in ethical terms *is* to think generally, searching always for agreement, or possible agreement, in the values involved. This is as true in the case of what I have referred to as private morality, the morality of conscience, as it is of public, or policy, morality. And, ethically speaking, when we value something, say honesty, or compassion, we are ready to claim that it is a lasting value, something that will continue to be valuable, not merely now but for the future.

It follows that, if we are interested in ethics at all, we can and must interest ourselves in handing on, from one generation to the next, the idea of ethics. If we believe in morality at all, then it is to moral *education* that we ought to give our most serious thought. For though humans may be capable by nature of adopting the ethical point of view, yet they do not always do so without being taught. This, then, is the practical issue with which I shall mainly concern myself in this final chapter.

In the last two chapters I have, I hope, disposed of two kinds of theory which seek to show the impossibility of ethics, to demonstrate, that is to say, that supposedly ethical considerations are necessarily fraudulent. The first of these theories was that there is no such thing as altruism, the second that there is no such thing as freedom, or responsibility for one's own actions. It may be argued that, at a practical level, it is very unlikely that a pure theory should ever influence people in the way they behave, or the way that they believe they and others should behave. Most people, when it comes to organising their lives, or deciding where their obligations lie, are profoundly uninterested in philosophy, or indeed in science. Nevertheless, theories have a way of spilling over into the practical concerns of life (which is, of course, what they are meant to do, for they are meant to be explanatory of life) and therefore people who might be hesitant to declare a theoretical attachment to a scientific or philosophical point of view may nevertheless be influenced by theorists, and may even be said to hold certain philosophical or scientific theories as unexamined assumptions, dictating their practical views, even if they are only partially aware of them. So it is time to look at some current beliefs which may make it difficult in practice to uphold ethical values, or to interest oneself in handing them on to others.

First there is the enemy of the ethical with which we are all familiar, that which spills over, as it were, from a form of determinism. The ramifications of this set of views are considerable, in that it tends to be a mixture of relatively vague theory and deeply held political beliefs.

I refer to the view that people cannot be held morally responsible for their bad behaviour because they are totally conditioned by their sociological circumstances. The doctrine is most prevalent, perhaps, and certainly most dangerous, when applied to children. But it may also be applied to adult criminals, with profound consequences for the theory and practice of punishment, its justification, purpose and efficacy. The vague theory lays down that someone who comes from a deprived background *cannot be blamed* for what he does, when that is agreed by common standards to be bad.

Since, as I have said, I shall mostly be concerned in this chapter with ethics in relation to education, I shall confine my remarks on this issue to the case of children. Now there is a sense in which we do not blame small children for behaving badly, or at least we do not hold them responsible for their behaviour. It is part of what we expect in children that at least from time to time they do outrageous things, or things that would be outrageous if perpetrated by adults. But we also hope that they may gradually learn to behave better; and it is for this reason that we tell them that what they have done is wrong, and we use in their hearing, and assuming their increasing understanding, the vocabulary of ethics, not about their behaviour alone but, inevitably, that of other people as well. For to employ the language of morals is to suggest to a child not simply that, I, his mother or his teacher, do not like what he is doing, or happen to wish he would stop doing it. It is to suggest, further, that no one ought to do that kind of thing. We use words like 'cruel' or 'unfair' or 'mean' as general descriptions of behaviour of a certain sort. We try to get the child to exercise his imaginative sympathy by asking how he would like it if someone deliberately ruined his game, as he has just ruined his brother's, or refused to share things which are supposed to be equally distributed. We teach him, gradually, to see what is common between himself and others, that if he does not like being teased, others will not like it either, and so through a whole range of kinds of behaviour. Being nice and being nasty are quite general concepts. And so the extent to which values are shared becomes gradually apparent in ethical contexts. Other people are drawn into the child's narrow sphere of awareness.

We may recognise, then, that a child from a certain kind of deprived background may not have come across this kind of reaction to what is generally held to be bad behaviour. In fact, in his immediate environment such behaviour may not be thought bad; or if it is, he may be more likely to be hit or shouted at than to hear the voice of moral disapproval when he has offended (for one of the worst forms of deprivation is the linguistic deprivation often suffered by children, who may hardly ever have actual conversation with adults). But to say this is not to say that a child, as he grows up, *cannot* learn what is wrong, and therefore, permanently, *cannot* be held responsible for what he does. It may be a matter of immense difficulty to teach him, and far more responsibility for doing so may fall on schools than they would like. Nevertheless one of the reasons why nursery education is of such enormous importance is its capacity to introduce the ideas of morality to a child, so that he begins to understand how to recognise temptation (the temptation, for instance, to get more for himself, or to bully those worse off than he) and to learn that temptation can be resisted. To suggest that it is impossible for a child from a deprived home to learn this kind of lesson is to diminish his humanity; it is to treat him as one might treat a dog or a horse. We may try, up to a point, to train these animals, but we will never hope to get them to understand that good behaviour is worth pursuing for its own sake. We can hardly hope to get them to prefer to do what they have been trained to do, that is to see the point of it. It may well be true to say that the evils of society, poverty, bad housing and widespread abuse of drugs and consequent crime all make for deprivation, and therefore to some extent cause the ignorance of, or indifference to, ethical considerations that we may see among children brought up among these evils. But to refer to these as total causal determinants is to deny that these particular human beings, individually, are capable of altruism, imagination and sympathy, the sources from which morality springs. And this is to forget their status as humans. It is not merely factually accurate, but morally imperative to treat children as morally competent, or capable of becoming so.

The belief that children from deprived backgrounds *cannot learn* about ethics, and therefore cannot be held responsible for what they do, is sometimes combined with the different view, equally class-orientated, that there are some things that they *should not be taught*. This was a theory prevalent in the 1960s and 1970s, less so now, fortunately. It derived in part from a paradoxical political theory which held that it was wrong to attempt to impose on children a kind of culture alien to them, and proper only to the dominant 'middle class white'. It involved a nervous attempt to respect all cultures equally. It derived as well from the influence of the American philosopher and educationalist, John Dewey, who held that in order to prepare American children for life in a democracy, the classroom must itself be a democratic place, the teacher just one among others, of equal status, not handing things down to his pupils from above. Relics of the theory are still to be found among some teachers of English, who regard the teaching of 'correct' English, or a 'canon' of literature, as unwarranted authoritarianism.

These two beliefs are not necessarily connected, but they are often held by the same people. Where they are, they seem to give rise to a total lack of hope for the children who are their objects. They will never be able to improve either their behaviour or their intellectual attainments. And so the so-called cycle of deprivation is inescapable. If a belief in the existence of morality depends on a belief that people may set new goals for themselves, and aspire to ideals, then this kind of watered-down determinism is an enemy of the ethical.

However, refusal to accept authoritative teaching, whether about ethics, language, history or any other aspect of the curriculum, has far more spreading roots than the egalitarianism I have just spoken of. It is firmly rooted in an encroaching relativism which is, I believe, the chief enemy of ethics. For the ethical point of view is, in Hume's words, 'a steady and general point of view'. Its generality and its implication of permanence and constancy are conveyed in all the vocabulary of morals. We have seen that the possibility of altruism, or unselfishness, is central to morality. To detach from one's judgement, as far as possible, the thought of one's own particular interest is essential both to the generality of that judgement, and to its steadiness, or indifference to time. If we can so detach ourselves then we may find, for example, that we morally admire the qualities in an enemy which are in fact harmful to ourselves. Relativism denies the possibility both of generality and of permanence. It reduces moral judgements to expressions of personal preference or personal interest, subject to fashionable prejudice, and not even aspiring to the 'steadiness' of truth.

The spread of moral relativism (itself by no means a new doctrine: Aristotle mentions, but rejects, it) may be partly due to the benign thought, of which we are often reminded, that we are a 'plural' society. There are many people living among us from different cultures and holding different religious beliefs. Teachers, in particular, are taught to be tolerant and understanding of different moral outlooks. It is held to be insensitive to insist on any one religious or ethical standpoint. William Dunning, in a remarkably frank article entitled 'Postmodernism and the construction of the divisible self', in the *British Journal of Aesthetics*, 1993, argues that 'the profusion of alternative modes of thinking and consciousness available to us today' makes it impossible to prefer one viewpoint to another. All are equally possible and equally 'justifiable'. We must not impose our own assumptions on others. From this springs the idea that all assumptions with regard to morality are equally 'valid' and this is the fundamental principle of relativism. What is good 'for you' may not be good 'for me'. Goodness is in the eye of the beholder. According to this doctrine it would be absurd to suggest that there was any such thing as moral truth. Even if one

were to describe the most evil political system imagin-
able, where a tyrannical government, say, tortured or
slaughtered its opponents, drove people from their homes,
took over the control of all material resources and en-
riched themselves at the expense of the people, one would
not be entitled to describe this regime as bad or wicked.
One would be entitled only to say that it seemed so to
oneself. Such radical relativism denies what I have asserted, namely that there are shared and permanent values,
arising from the nature of humanity itself. (One may note
in passing that the evil political system I have just described would most probably be universally condemned
as in breach of human rights. This shows the truth of what
I have already argued, that to talk in terms of rights sounds
objective and factual; it seems not to involve putting
forward a moral opinion of one's own, but to appeal to
some pre-existing law which can be referred to dispas-
sionately. Ethical relativists seek at all costs to avoid
expressing genuine moral opinions. Their fear is that they
be thought 'judgemental'.) Relativists who derive their
views immediately from a requirement of tolerance may
support their fear of dogmatism, of laying down the moral
law, by an appeal to a yet more general relativism, which
goes by the name of postmodernism. This is the theory
that truth itself, not only in the context of morality, is a
nonsensical concept. There is, it is held, an infinity of
different ways of looking at any one object. In the context
of the visual arts, for example, there is no one privileged
way of seeing. Every object has innumerable facets, and

if we seek to represent an object, in art, there is no one mode of representation that is more valid or 'truthful' than any other. Such extreme relativism can be traced back, perhaps, to Nietzsche who held that the primary motivating force in the world was the Will to Power. Any set of beliefs is simply an instrument to be used in the service of this will.

The fashionable (or once fashionable) French intellectual, Michel Foucault (1926-1984), a follower of Nietzsche, held that throughout the history of ideas, there have been a series of different 'knowledges', or 'archaeologies', all of them motivated by the wish to dominate, by marginalising certain groups of people. Thus supposedly objective science was called in aid to identify those who were ill, or mad, or criminal, or sexually deviant. All such descriptions are invested with a false objectivity in order to justify the oppression of those so described. In the same spirit, certain feminists hold that the attempt to adopt, or impose, a single point of view, to search for a truth which is true for everyone, is the outcome of this dominating will. Thus there are postmodernist women painters who argue that to continue to deploy the traditional techniques of perspective is to succumb to an entrenched white male view of a world which is in fact essentially shifting and multiple, containing no stable elements, no properly privileged viewpoint, no absolute facts, and no continuing or shared values.

Postmodernism is a gift to radical feminism, in every sphere. It reinforces the view that what seems to be sought in studying, for example physics, or chemistry or biology, is a single truth about the world which will show things as they are. But physicists, chemists and biologists in the past have been predominantly male; therefore their perspective on the world has been a masculine perspective, which cannot possibly represent the whole truth, nor indeed is the idea of 'the whole truth' coherent. Everything depends on whose voice is heard. What is now needed is a women's physics, or a women's chemistry or biology, invented by women and taught to women. If asked what these sciences would be like, the answer is that it is impossible to tell, since women have never been given the chance to invent them, free from the dominating orthodoxy imposed by men. But it should not be thought that these new sciences would reveal more of *the truth about the world* than the old. That there is a 'truth about the world' is, it is held, an archaic bit of mythology. The new sciences would at best reveal another truth, a truth 'for women'. Such is the doctrine of relativism, enshrined in radical feminism.

But feminism is only one example of the postmodernist denial of truth. As I have suggested, the scepticism of Foucault is another. Such scepticism is unlike the old philosophical scepticism of Descartes, who sought to put in doubt everything that he had hitherto taken for granted as true, in order to retain the real truths which, he thought, with the greatest efforts of scepticism in the world, he could not doubt. In contrast, the scepticism of postmodernism is more akin to cynicism. No 'truth' is to be trusted, because every truth put forward is the outcome of some vested interest, the interest in power.

And there is a yet more radical and pervasive version of postmodernism. This is the theory that what we say or write is not even meant to have any reference to a world outside itself, to be 'true of' it. It is just words. I find this proposition exceptionally difficult to understand, and this is not only, though it is partly, because those who put forward such views generally express them in words deliberately intended to obfuscate and confuse. It is largely because such propositions seem themselves to claim to be true (as indeed do most assertions that we make, whether theoretical or practical), and therefore the theory seems intrinsically self-contradictory. It is difficult to avoid the conclusion that those who hold it, or profess to do so, are motivated by a desire not only to confuse, but to shock with the boldness of their paradoxes. Jacques Derrida, for example, regards the existence of a 'text' (increasingly and irritatingly used in certain educational circles to mean not merely a written text, but words spoken, or images offered in, for example, advertisements, or news bulletins) as simply an invitation for interpretation. Any interpretation is permissible, and each is as valid as the rest. The question whether the text itself says something that is true of the world does not arise, because there is nothing outside it that it is supposed to represent. Interpretation is 'play' (see Derrida, *Speech and Phenomena*, North-West University Press). In a similar spirit, the American philosopher, Richard Rorty, a fervent admirer both of Nietzsche and of Derrida, regards philosophy itself, especially epistemology, as mistaken if it believes that it can approach towards any truth about the world. Instead, it should regard itself as engaged in a perpetual conversation, its aim not veracity but simply to keep the conversation going, whatever is said (see *Philosophy and the Mirror of Nature*, Blackwell, 1980). It is Derrida, however, who has been influential over a number of academics in Cambridge, especially those interested in literary criticism and the limits of legitimate interpretation. (There was a notable row in Cambridge in the early 1990s when Derrida was given an honorary degree. I myself had just left Cambridge at this time; otherwise I should have felt obliged to resign from the Council of Senate, then the governing body of the university, and responsible for the list of honorands.) One of the Cambridge academics most strongly influenced by postmodernism in general, Derrida and Rorty in particular, is the popular theologian, Don Cupitt. He has written a number of short, rhetorical books, putting forward the view that there is no such thing as a world 'outside the text'. For example, in his book *What is a Story?* (SCM, 1991), he argues that, whereas in traditional philosophy, starting from Plato, a story might be true, or it might be an allegory, or a parable, the vehicle for timeless and unchanging truth, now there is no one who believes in truth, least of all in timeless or unchanging truth. Instead we believe that what we may please to call the truth is actually created as we go along, by the telling of stories:

'Another story, another truth.' He writes: 'Truth is no longer something out there; it is a way with words. The preacher, interpreter or artist is now making truth in the telling of a tale … The interpreter is no longer just a servant of the truth, but has become someone whose job is the endless production of truth' (op. cit., p. 23). (It is no wonder that literary critics may begin to get ideas above their station.) And finally, in summing up his thoughts, he announces that 'story structures time and the world and keeps darkness and death at bay, at least for a while. We are listening to Scheherazade again, putting off death by listening to tales through the night. Narrative, only narrative conquers darkness and the void.' (op. cit., p. 80). It would be held to be extraordinarily philistine, I suppose, to enquire in the light of such rhetoric, whether literally all narrative has these powers, and whether it is actually the case that we no longer believe in truth. Postmodernists never make it clear whether their 'texts' are to include such mundane items as the minutes of the previous meeting, or an account of which way you drove between Oxford and Cambridge. But if what they say they believe is really to be believed, then presumably boring truths as well as those that are elevated should be included, and we can interpret these tedious narratives in any way we like. It is all a game.

Now it may be argued that this kind of galloping relativism, concerned as it is with the theory of knowledge and with the possibility of knowledge itself, though its influence may be harmful to academic integrity, to scholarship and to science, is not relevant to ethics. But I believe that this argument would be mistaken. Let us assume, to make them more plausible, that the theories of postmodernism are not meant to apply to shopping lists or police evidence or ordinary long boring stories, but only to the 'texts' of history, literature and science; yet the academic virtues, concern with evidence, honesty, the effort not to mislead, are all virtues that can be pursued in circles much wider than the strictly academic. Those directly influenced by Derrida, Rorty or Cupitt may themselves exercise a far wider influence. University students do not remain in their universities for ever; and when they emerge they become ordinary humans, engaged in various professional activities. If what they have been taught, implicitly or explicitly, is that there is no such thing as truth; that it does not matter what interpretation you put on things as long as you keep talking; that there is no difference between an account of something based on evidence and one that is mere fancy; that any story will do as long as it keeps your audience awake, then, in the ordinary, non-philosophical sense of the term, they have become irresponsible.

Moreover if these 'academic' values are denied, on the grounds that there is no such thing as truth, how much more will it seem that relativism must rule in the case of more obviously ethical, non-academic values, where, as I have argued, there is positive pressure in favour of pluralism and the non-existence of truth or falsity. If there are no such things as agreed facts then surely we can even less pretend that there are agreed values.

Thus it seems that the somewhat absurd and esoteric doctrines of postmodernism may have a creeping and insidious effect, and especially so in schools, where teachers may find themselves bewildered by their own half-articulate principles that they must not be dogmatic, they must not presume that there are any disinterested or unbiased arguments, and above all they must not be 'judgemental'. Universal scepticism, if this means an openness to new ideas, an ability to criticise what has been taken for granted, and a constant demand for good evidence, may be an excellent qualification for teaching; but universal cynicism is not. If you do not believe in anything, then what are you to teach?

Cynicism has two wings. One is the failure to distinguish between genuine attempts to tell the truth, between candour and honesty, on the one hand, and propaganda and special pleading on the other. For this failure, politicians have much to answer. Despite all calls for 'open government', it is increasingly difficult to believe what any politician says in public. The unconcealed existence of so-called spin doctors entails that we are all perfectly aware that every message is slanted, every political utterance scrutinised and manipulated for its presentational effectiveness, for all the world as if it were part of an advertising campaign. But at least advertising, though it may have more effect on us than we should like, openly avows that it is trying to sell us something. If we buy the product, we have, in the end, no one but ourselves to blame; and at least advertisers can often justify their trade by claiming that they convey information about new products. Propaganda, on the other hand, though according to the original sense of the term it was open, like advertising, seeking to sell the true faith, is now essentially hidden. It passes itself off as straight information. Yet, at the same time, we all know about the spin doctors in the background. Is it any wonder that we are confused, and fall back into cynicism?

But cynicism is not just a barren intellectual attitude. For its other wing is moral. If we cannot identify any factual truths, still less can we identify truths about values. The moral cynic does not believe that there is anything ultimately worth pursuing. We may be conned into thinking that some things are better than others, some ways of life more noble, less demeaning; but in fact to believe this is to succumb to a trick. The first cynic of this kind to be described in Western literature was Thrasymachus, one of the participants in Plato's dialogue, *The Republic*, who enunciated the view that justice, or morality, was nothing but the interest of the stronger, a system imposed on the weak to keep them in order. A latter-day cynic was John McKie, whom I mentioned earlier, who held that we had invented (or reinvented) such concepts as that of duty and obligation and kept them in existence artificially, once the sanctions of religion held no credence. Nietzsche was, of course, the arch-cynic.

To be a cynic is, simply, depressing. Intellectually, it

does not matter what you say. Even if you personally retain a belief that truth is different from falsehood, there is no hope that you will be believed, so you may as well conceal the truth, manipulate the facts, invent the evidence. At least you may have some fun, become rich and famous, a leader in your field. Morally, since there is nothing that is actually worth pursuing, your life is without meaning. It does not matter what you do. If there are no long-term goals that are truly valuable, you might as well pursue short-term advantage, and get what you can while you can. It has no significance in the long run.

It seems to me that a lot of children emerge from school cynical and depressed in this sort of way. And with all the talk about our plural society, and the implied multiplicity of moral standards, the real difference is between those who have some moral standards, some belief that it is worth pursuing the good, whatever particular vision of the good is before them, and those who have none.

One recourse to combat the dismalness of cynicism is to turn, instead, to fanatical fundamentalism, political, or, more probably, religious. The trouble with fundamentalism is that, while it may bring comfort and a sense of purpose to the lives of its adherents, it is essentially blind and anti-rational. Most fundamentalists derive their beliefs from a text, whose doctrines are their inspiration. But a text, though in reality subject to different interpretations, is likely, in the flight from cynicism, to be taken literally, as propounding an unchanging set of truths, which make up the whole truth. To accept a text wholesale does not admit the legitimacy of critical scepticism, of the kind I have contrasted with cynicism. It therefore leads inevitably to dogma and conflict, and to claims of more certainty than the complexities of human life actually warrant. It is the enemy of imagination and therefore of sympathy. The more depressing a life without any beliefs appears, a life without the concept of either truth or value, the more understandable it is to turn to the security of absolute beliefs, however irrational. This is a real danger in a 'plural' society.

Yet fundamentalism is not the only way of escape. The other way is to believe that some things are true, others false, and that among the truths is the truth that some forms of society are better than others. It is better for humans to live in a society where the laws are respected, where crime is not only prohibited by law but also thought wrong, where there is respect for justice and for the rights of others, where what I have designated as public morality is the norm. That such a form of society is better is not merely a matter of opinion. It is a fact, derived from the nature of humans themselves. However, to teach such lessons to children is difficult. It is partly because they are not interested in abstract concepts such as that of 'society' or 'government'. But in any case the lessons may seem especially vulnerable to the Thrasymachean, cynical response. Obviously those in authority, government, police, teachers, will teach the lesson of obedience to the law, respect for authority, the sanctity of rights and the rest. It is profoundly in their own interests to do so. Obviously those who possess property will teach the evils of theft, those with financial interests the wrongfulness of fraud. The whole system is set up and kept in being for the protection of vested interests. The more glaring the difference between those who are affluent and those who are virtually without anything, and the more frequently members of government or the police are found themselves to be corrupt, the stronger the attractions of this kind of cynicism must seem. It is often suggested that there should be lessons in 'citizenship' at school, that is, I suppose, lessons in public morality. I deeply doubt the utility of such lessons. Instead I believe we must start at the beginning, and help children to discover that there is such a thing as private morality, the ethics of conscience and of possible ideals, a system within which they can personally and individually set goals for themselves, and which will help to give significance to their lives.

So how is this to be done? First of all, from the earliest age teachers (wherever possible in collaboration with parents) must unashamedly use the language of ethics. They must say that things are wrong or cruel or dishonest; or that they are brave, kind or good. And these things must be the things that children themselves do, they must relate to actual behaviour in the classroom or playground. Even the youngest children must feel that they are involved in ethical alternatives; they themselves can be good or bad. They are subject, as we all are, to temptations but they can overcome them, and when they do, they are becoming good. John Dewey was determined that the classroom must be a microcosm of a democratic state; in one way, he was right. A classroom should be a microcosm of the boat we are all in. It should show the human predicament, that things can go well or ill, but that they will go better if we think of others than ourselves. But in another way, as I have suggested, he was wrong. For he thought that democracy entailed that the teacher had a status no different from that of the pupils themselves. Everyone is equal, and nothing must be handed down by an 'authority'. But in the matter of ethics, the teacher must *know* what is right and what is wrong, must confidently draw the distinction for her pupils, and in the matter of their behaviour, must give praise or blame to what deserves it. Simply in virtue of being grown-up, the teacher has this authority. And of course she will teach largely by example: fairness, truthfulness, kindness, an interest in other people, a willingness to put herself out, and postpone her own interests to those of others, the faithful keeping of promises. All these things will be observed by her pupils and increasingly relied on. Of course such virtues and the words in which they may be referred to will be familiar to some of her pupils and not to others. But even for those children whose parents make use of all these words and by their behaviour exemplify and encourage all these virtues, there are moral lessons to be learned at nursery and primary school when perhaps for the first time they come in close daily contact with people other than their families, who are unlike themselves, and where they are not the centre of attention. Children from close and loving families sometimes find this hard to get used to. Education is not all compensation, or making up for lack.

Important though such explicit ethical teaching is, I would give as high a priority to the development of a child's imagination, indeed without this a child will have no safeguard against the deadening cynicism which is the enemy of morality. It is only through his imagination that a child can learn to place himself in a world with others and begin to recognise that there are permanent values in that world, in which he and others are equally interested.

Of course different children may find imaginative excitement in different things. For no apparent reason, one may develop a craze for birds, another for old cars, another for rocks and stones. And the nature of a craze is to make a child feel that there is infinitely more in the subject than he yet knows, that it could engage his attention for ever, and he still would not have got to the end of it. Even if the child in question in the end goes off birds, and on to something else, still to have had that excitement about a subject is to know what it is like to have one's imagination fully engaged. In its small way, it is like having been in love.

But for all children, whether or not they are subject to crazes, there is one central way to engage and develop their imagination, and that is through the reading or telling of stories. For stories present themselves not as mere narrative, one thing happening after another, but as encapsulating values, which are permanent, intelligible and above all shared. C.S. Lewis, in his essay, 'On Stories'

(C.S. Lewis, *Of This and Other Worlds*, Collins, 1982), argued, for example, that the story of Jack the Giant Killer conveyed as its central value a species of fear, the fear of the monstrous, which cannot be conveyed except in a story, and which is immediately intelligible. The story has a point, and this point could not be made without the idea of giants. It is not that we are familiar, in real life, with an actual fear of giants; but that we know this *kind* of fear (and perhaps children especially do) and we understand, albeit obscurely, that it is universal. (Lewis himself wrote the most memorable evocation of this very fear in the course of his children's book, *The Silver Chair*.) Consider, again, a story on which I was brought up, as were all my children, who used to demand that it be read again and again, the story of the Little Old Woman Who Lived in a Vinegar Bottle. She lived in her bottle extremely frugally; and one day she rescued a fairy from extinction. The fairy, in gratitude, gave her a wish, and promised he would come back if ever she wanted anything more. The old woman wished for a cottage to live in, and got it. But then her ambitions grew and grew. She repeatedly summoned back the fairy, demanding new clothes, a maid, a horse, a carriage and two horses, every time explaining that she could not live, in her new state, without the desired object. In the end, predictably, the fairy lost patience and said, 'You discontented little old woman: the more you have, the more you want. Go back to your vinegar bottle,' and all the good things disappeared. The moral of this tale may not have been very elevated; but it was plain and familiar. The badness of bad behaviour shone out, and every time it was read, the punch-line gave equal pleasure. Consider, again, the parable of the Good Samaritan, a rich story indeed. The Samaritan, not the sort of person from whom much might be expected, unlike the people of better reputation, not only took pity on the victim in the ditch, but to his own inconvenience took him to an inn, and paid for his food out of his own pocket. He need not have done any of these things: but he did, out of sheer goodness.

The enormous merit of stories as a way of conveying values is that even when the plot is totally familiar from reading and rereading, you can come back again to savour and find more in the *idea* which is its central point. So far from its being true that narrative is nothing but words, it is on the contrary exactly what Cupitt denied, the vehicle for timeless truth. The values conveyed are permanent and to be grasped by everyone. Stories simplify and exaggerate; for children they comfort by making clear the difference between the nice and the nasty, the good and the bad, the hero and the coward, and this is true of all stories that children love, whatever their style or provenance.

The sense of the continuity and the timelessness of the ideas that are at the centre of stories, ideas such as the idea of fear, of grasping discontent, or of pure charity which I have called values, is related to the fact that these ideas are shared. The story is told for everyone, and is significant for everyone. I am not suggesting that ethical values never change. We know that they do, and, for example, it may be quite difficult for children of the twentieth and twenty-first centuries to make sense of some of the ideas (say ideas of rigid class distinctions, or of the supreme value attached to virginity for girls) which lie at the centre of many novels of the nineteenth century. But they will find this difficult only if they have never been taught to think historically, and to exercise their imagination in a specifically historical mode. And we can understand history only because there is enough that is common, ethically, between the past and the present to enable us to see what the point was, what the fuss was about, and how the essential virtues and vices, those which determine our relations with other people, remain the same, even in these different expressions. In the matter of sexual morality, for instance, though what is acceptable and discussable has changed, nevertheless there are fundamental values which have not changed, and which are relevant in any relation between one person and others, values such as love and commitment, honesty and pleasure, friendship and loyalty, and, on the other hand, exploitation, selfishness, greed and the inability to love.

Because such values are permanent and shared, children can begin to understand that there are things that are, and always have been, intrinsically worth doing, and other things of which one must be ashamed. School is a place where a child, like Aristotle's young men, can practise doing what is good, and can thus come to prefer it to doing what is bad. And it is not only in the sphere of ethics that this is true. Moral values are not the only values where, as a child learns to distinguish the good from the bad, he acquires a source of permanent significance in his life; he begins to be able to set himself new goals, and discover a point in doing things well rather than badly. Thus to teach a child the difference between a shoddy and a creditable performance, as an actor, a singer or an instrumentalist, as a painter or a potter, is to introduce him to values that are, like ethical values, superficially changing but fundamentally timeless, and capable of being shared.

When educationalists or curriculum-designers talk of the need for 'moral and spiritual education', I think, and hope, that this is what they mean. There is sometimes an outcry against such talk, on the grounds that 'spiritual' must mean religious, and children, unless their parents specifically choose this for them, should not be taught the dogmas of religion. In reply to this I would argue that religion is one expression of the 'spiritual', an expression which people may find of immense significance, and perhaps indispensable in their lives. For the stories taught in teaching a religion contain ideas which may seem to lose their point if stripped from their religious context. Though religions must speak in metaphors and symbols (for even the most religiously dogmatic seldom claim to have seen God face to face), yet the metaphors may seem impossible to translate into any other mode. But in truth any teaching is 'spiritual' which opens a child's eyes to the position he as a human being occupies in the universe. In this sense, a lesson in palaeontology or geology, in biology, ecology or chemistry may be spiritual, insofar as the pupil may gradually learn where he stands in the history of the world, what he can try to find out, what his responsibilities are.

A good school, then, will produce ambitious pupils who want to go on with what they have started. Whatever they do, they will want to do it well. As they more and more clearly see the implications of being human, they will want, as Aristotle might have put it, to be good specimens of humanity. In ethical terms they will want to be good. Without this underlying private want, they cannot be relied on to try for the ethically best in the public sphere. The morality that lies behind all efforts to improve things in the world at large, to defend human rights, to pass generally acceptable laws, to seek peace and justice, is essentially that of private standard-setting, and of private ideals to be pursued. And this is why children from the earliest age, and in the most trivial and domestic and unheroic contexts, must learn that, being human, they are subject to temptation, and being human, they can, if they want to, triumph.

Index